- MY ULTIMATE -
ZOJIRUSHI
Rice Cooker Cookbook

*100 Surprisingly Delicious Instant Pot Style Recipes with
Illustrations for your Micom NS-TSC Rice Cooker*

By

Elizabeth Daniels

*Pan Pacific press
Santa Monica, CA*

CUSTOMER REVIEWS

"This book provides nutrition info with each recipe. That's a huge plus for me (and a potential reduction in my plus-size ;) With such a wide variety of recipes, knowing the amounts of calories, fat, carbs, etc. makes it really helpful and easy to know exactly what I'm eating. Provides a surprisingly wide variety of tasty meals. Loving this book!" - Melanie R.

"I was surprised you could cook an entire roasted chicken in this machine. It's way more than a just a rice cooker and steamer. Thanks for making this. These kinds of foodie discoveries are really fun." – Tom S.

"This book covers a wide reach with some seriously great recipes. My husband L O V E D The Bar-B-Q ribs (they were tasty) I fell for the Dijon Chicken with mushrooms and we are just getting started. I've never tired rice pudding before so I'm looking forward to that and a lot of other meals I've never known how to cook" - Rachel C

"Great for beginners! I like the clear instructions, serving sizes and nutritional info...the range of recipes is impressive and helps me keep my family of 5 looking forward to dinner time." - Liz E.

LEGAL NOTICE

PAN PACIFIC PRESS

Published in the United States of America by Pan Pacific Press

www.Pan-PacificPress.com

Want a FREE Cookbook?

Then join the
Book Review Club!

(It's Free for readers like you)

Get your first free cookbook today
at this link:

www.JoinTheBookReviewClub.com/a3

TABLE OF CONTENTS

1

WHY BUY THIS BOOK!

Save Time with Our Illustrated Quick Start Guide

Kitchen appliances have come a long way since rice cookers your grandma used to sit on top of a boiling pot of water on the stove. You can now program electric rice cookers and warmers with the touch of a button and walk away. With our Quick Start Guide, you won't have to read through endless confusing instructions we all skip through anyway. You can enjoy time without watching the stove because today they do all the work for you. You'll be able to easily understand the digital controls, parts, and instructions, and be on your way to healthy, fun family meals in no time. The best part about this book is how we'll show you the Zojirushi Rice Cooker and Warmer doesn't only cook rice—you can whip up delicious one-pot meals and gourmet delights right in the comfort of your own kitchen in a fraction of the time it takes to cook in a traditional oven. And of course, we make sure you'll get your Zojirushi to create the most perfectly fluffy and delicious rice in just half the time.

Unbiased Real-World Instructions and Recipes You Won't Find in Any Zojirushi

With this book, you'll get decadent and delicious meals having your taste buds think you're eating dishes prepared by a gourmet chef. You'll find handy customized recipes that help you easily convert cups in lieu of only using the smaller measuring cup that comes with the Zojirushi. All the meals are easy to prepare with detailed, easy-to-follow instructions that won't have you curious, which settings to use let alone how long to cook meat and rice at the same time. You won't find tips and tricks like how to crisp meals inside a rice cooker in just any cookbook. With the Zojirushi rice cooker, also gone are the long cooking times that old school rice cooker and the days of boring one pot meals. This cookbook has got you covered.

100 Amazing Recipes Not Found in Other Cookbooks

This book also offers you 100 amazing recipes not found in any other Zojirushi Rice Cooker and Warmer cookbook. These unique and easy to prepare recipes to elevate your breakfast, lunch, dinner, and desserts to a whole new level. If you love one pot, easy meals that can put dinner on the table with the push of one button this cookbook is for you. You'll learn how to cook rice and meat at the same time, so you're cooking time is cut in half. Prepare healthy dishes and meals for your family with the power of steam. We'll also include Kid-Friendly recipes that will have the little ones wanting to get in on all the quick kitchen fun. From comforting meats, soups and stews to refreshing salads and decadent desserts—this book offers you 100 amazing recipes that will have everyone in the family wanting to use the Zojirushi Rice Cooker and Warmer.

Pro Tips to Get the Most from Your Zojirushi Rice Cooker and Warmer

Not only will you get detailed, easy-to-use instructions and 100 mouthwatering recipes—you'll get our pro tips and tricks to help you get the most out of your Zojirushi Rice Cooker and Warmer. You'll be surprised at what and just how much this amazing appliance can do! This book will teach you how to cook meals for later, saving you even more time. These pro tips help you find all the things not normally associated with rice cookers, so you make the perfect meal every time. Whether pressurized or not, we put together the most comprehensive set of tips included with the 100 recipes of some succulently, surprising things you can make in the Zojirushi Rice Cooker and Warmer.

How to Avoid Common Mistakes and Start Cooking Like a Pro

This book is so comprehensive and thorough, that you'll learn how to avoid common mistakes and start cooking like a pro in no time. No more burning or scorching your food you walked away from! With the Zojirushi Rice Cooker and Warmer, you will not only learn how to cook perfect rice, this book will teach you how to avoid mistakes when cooking other grains like brown and multigrain rice, as well as quinoa. You learn how to perfectly steam meat, as well as kid-friendly pasta and fun recipes. You'll never scorch your favorite fish, pork, chicken, or beef again. You'll even learn how to keep those gooey, cheesy one-pot meals from sticking to the lid in your Zojirushi Rice Cooker and Warmer.

The Most Comprehensive Book Written for the Zojirushi Rice Cooker and Food Steamer

Looking to cook up the most healthy, nutritious meals on the planet? You'll be able to do just that and save time when you use the Zojirushi Rice Cooker and Warmer. In this book, with this product, you'll find more simple-to-use instructions, guides, pro tips, recipes and Zojirushi knowledge than all of those other more complex books and cookers. We break things down and make them so super simple that even your oldest family member will be able to use this kitchen appliance with ease. Not only will you get all of the information needed in a simple, easy to use guide—you'll get 100 mouthwatering recipes to help you master your Zojirushi Rice Cooker and Warmer.

Gourmet Tips to Cook Perfectly Cooked, Delicious Rice

Of course, you won't just get 100 amazing recipes—we've included scrumptious gourmet tips to have you cooking perfectly delicious rice every time you use your Zojirushi Rice Cooker and Warmer! Not only rice, but think soups, salads, stews, and delicious one pot meals. You'll learn how to perfect sushi rice, make your own multigrain rice dishes, and just how to use them in your favorite salads, soups, and meals. You'll learn how to elevate meals for breakfast like yogurt parfaits and french toast. That's right you can even cook breakfast like yogurt, french toast, and pancakes in your Zojirushi Rice Cooker and Warmer.

Several Paleo, Diabetic-Friendly, and Gluten-Free Recipes Included

One of the most amazing details about the Zojirushi Rice Cooker and Warmer is all the healthy meals you'll be able to serve up! Our recipes will have gourmet tips that help you whip up paleo, diabetic-friendly, and gluten-free recipes too! We'll help you learn easy conversion tips that help you transform your favorite dietary lifestyle into a foodie's dream. With this book on the Zojirushi Rice Cooker and Warmer, you'll be able to understand just how to convert ingredients in order to make delicious vegan and vegetarian dishes in your cooker. That's just how comprehensive this book is when it comes to mastering food prepared in the Zojirushi Rice Cooker and Warmer.

2

ALL ABOUT PROGRAMMABLE
PRESSURE COOKING

A Brief History of the Programmable Rice cooker

Historians haven't quite figured out exactly who invented this genius kitchen appliance, but on January 9th, 1991, the Chinese scientist, Mr. Yong-Guang Wang, filed the first electric rice cooker patent. While this is the best way to cook instant, fluffy, restaurant-quality rice directly in your own home, the Zojirushi Rice Cooker and Warmer is a multi-dish device that doesn't just focus on 'rice & steaming'. This electric rice cooker offers you several ways to cook food at once such as simmering, braising, slow cooking, warming, and stewing by using different combinations of cooking temperature, pressure and cooking times which has since lead to the new era of electric rice cookers and the Zojirushi Rice Cooker and Warmer.

The Immense Variety of Dishes Programmable Rice Cookers Create!

You can whip up quick and easy breakfast in the morning, so you can curb your morning stop on your commute and start the day with more healthy meals like yogurt parfait, old-fashioned oatmeal, veggie frittatas, quiche, and even hard-boiled eggs. Lunch is made much more simple with this electric rice cooker too! You can easily create fast healthy dishes like Buddha Bowls, Pad Thai, Jacket Potatoes, and Chicken Tacos. Dinners, desserts and snacks, and beyond are all made more simple with the Zojirushi Rice Cooker and Warmer. Think Pho, Chocolate Lava Cake, Mac N' Cheese, Chili Dogs and Whole Roasted Chicken. All fast, healthy, and absolutely delicious!

Health Benefits of Cooking with the Zojirushi Rice Cooker and Warmer

The Zojirushi Rice Cooker and Warmer offer you a vast array of health benefits. Not only will you be cooking clean and only adding the oil necessary to keep the dish from sticking, you'll learn how to really make each dish in the healthiest cooking style possible. Electric rice cookers cut preservatives, GMOs, and other unhealthy additives. You'll be cooking food as naturally as possible, just like pro chefs. Pressure cooking is also diet friendly. Not just any diet, but great for people who are trying to lower their cholesterol and blood pressure. Amazing for anyone wanting to cut fat and sugar. Vegetarians, Vegans, Paleo can all create delicious meals with the Zojirushi Rice Cooker and Warmer. Along with rice, you can steam veggies for paleo, vegan or carb-watching diets—as well as meats, pasta, and other delicious grains like quinoa.

Why Pro Chefs Use Programmable Rice Cookers

You can perfectly cook like a pro chef right in your own home with because it's pressurized all of the different flavors are infused into the food and really seals in the flavor. Totally transcends the flavor of each meal you cook at home. The cooking time goes from the traditional 30 to 10 minutes on each meal. Minimal cleaning and super fun to use at home, the electric rice cooker is loved by pro chefs, as well as busy parents and students love programmable rice cookers. Professional chefs love the quickness of cooking with a rice cooker and the fact that you can taste all of the Zojirushi and flavors infused into your meal. Technology has made it so you can cook like a pro chef right at home!

The Difference Between an Electric Rice Cooker and Pressure Cooker

The electric rice cooker and pressure cooker usually look almost exactly the same. Many people often wonder exactly what the difference is when it comes to cooking with both appliances. While they both cook food at an incredibly quick rate of time, they are very different. Both appliances cook using steam, but that's the only thing these two have in common. The electric rice cooker uses a heating coil or pad with an inner pan and lid. Sometimes they come with steaming baskets, sometimes they don't. Rice is cooked using liquid, like water, that evaporates and turns into steam that the rice absorbs and cause the rice to become fluffy and soft. The Zojirushi Rice Cooker is similar to the pressure cooker but is designed with a sensor on the lid that is sealable so steam cannot escape and cooks the food with a combination of heat and pressure. Zojirushi is simple and has less buttons to figure out than most programmable pressure cookers. Most electric rice cookers are programmable and often easier to use and can cook a more vast array of tantalizing meals and scrumptious dishes.

3

HOW TO USE YOUR ZOJIRUSHI COOKER

How to Get Started In 2 Minutes!

Add rice. Add at least 1 cup of water. Push a button. That's how simple it is to get started using your Zojirushi Rice Cooker and Warmer. Use the power button to get started. Make sure you read all of the instructions carefully before the first use. Make sure your Zojirushi is on a flat surface with nothing underneath the stainless steel surface! Be sure to use your Zojirushi Rice Cooker and Warmer only on a level, dry and heat-resistant surface. Wipe any water or residue off the outside and surface of the heating plate; that way you have zero corrosion or noise during cooking and rice cooks properly. Secure the inner lid in place by pushing it into the fixtures found on both sides at the bottom of the outer lid and push up until it is secure. Next, pull the inner lid knobs towards you that are found on the top. Place the inner pan in the main body, secure the lid closed, and press cook/reheat to set your time or choose the rice option you are cooking. When the cook time is complete the Zojirushi will shift to keep-warm mode.

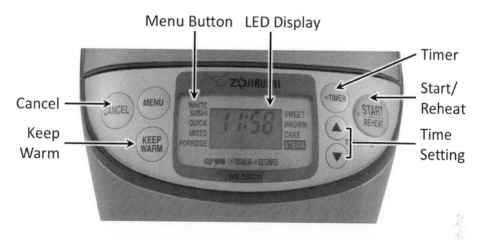

Overview of Buttons, Timer, and Settings

The buttons and timers are super easy to learn. With every recipe, you'll learn just how to cook each meal to perfection. There's a button for quick cooking white rice automatically. One for cooking fluffy, delicious brown rice and grains that require longer cooking times. The mixed button is great for steaming vegetables and other delicious main dishes. While the sushi rice, porridge, and other buttons can help you cook the most tantalizing meals when you are super-busy or aren't even at home. You can also use the keep warm button to keep food fresh and hot when your dinner guests haven't arrived or dinner is postponed. You really can get started in two minutes with the Zojirushi Rice Cooker and Warmer—for delicious, healthy, pro chef style meals right at home. The best part about the Zojirushi are all the accessories that come with this rice cooker. No other model on the market offers you such a simple way to cook delicious rice – even rice that is not pre-washed is delicious and fluffy in no time with Zojirushi.

Overview of How to Cook Rice, Soups, Stews, Vegetables, and More

Rice is easy to cook using the 13-step process below. Many soup and stew recipes will require you to use the timer function in order to avoid burning the soup. You'll want to set the time that each dish needs to steam. The Zojirushi Rice Cooker and Warmer will begin to countdown once water reaches a boil. Then it will shut off once time has elapsed. The best part about this rice cooker is that it will automatically switch over to keep warm once the rice is finished cooking. That way you know you get perfect, fluffy rice every single time you cook. Soups will never scorch again. Dishes won't stick to lids or burn. Vegetables won't wilt but be cooked to steamed perfection.

How to Clean and Store Your Zojirushi Rice Cooker and Warmer

Allow the appliance to cool before starting the cleaning process. Unplug your Zojirushi Rice Cooker and Warmer from the electric outlet before cleaning. On occasion, there may be residue in the bottom of your Zojirushi Rice Cooker and Warmer. While this is almost always unavoidable, you can easily clean the appliance in no time at all. Simply pour a few inches of water into the bottom of the Zojirushi Rice Cooker and Warmer. Cycle it through cooking again on steam. The boiling water will loosen up any remaining residue and help you easily wipe it clean with a damp cloth. Do not use harsh abrasive cleaners, scouring pads or products that are not considered safe to use on non-stick coatings, as this will discolor or ruin the inner pan and accessories. Simply store your rice cooker in a dry place.

Optimal Sizes of Food, How to Time and Avoid Overcooking

Food sizes can vary, and it is especially useful to follow the recipes to the exact measurement. This will help you avoid overfilling and overcooking your meals. The timer and cooking specifications on each recipe will also help you avoid overcooking food. Tools that come with the Zojirushi Rice Cooker and Warmer like the steam tray, spatula, and measuring cup can come in very handy. A ribbed spatula is great when lifting rice out of your rice cooker to keep it from falling all over the place. A great pro tip: add a 1/2 tsp. Olive oil to rice to avoid bubbling over. Remember that food expands as you cook in your Zojirushi Rice Cooker and Warmer so never fill it more than 1/2 full or past the maximum fill line.

Do not fill over this line, because food expands while cooking.

Marinating and Prepping Dishes/How to Store Leftovers

Marinating and prepping dishes beforehand are a great way to cook healthy meals in no time. The Zojirushi Rice Cooker and Warmer are great for making 3-4 serving size meals. Remember to reduce the size of traditional soup or stew recipes for 94-ounce pots and rice cookers. 64 ounce resealable containers are great for the Zojirushi Rice Cooker and Warmer. This size container holds 3-4 servings and is perfect for freezing ingredients to quick cook from frozen. If you don't have time to put all of the ingredients together, you can pick a day to meal prep. Freeze in 64-ounce containers and cook a delicious, healthy family meal in no time. When storing leftovers, just place them in resealable containers and refrigerate for up to 72 hours or freeze for up to 14 days.

Things to Avoid

Recipes included in this book are easy to follow. Some recipes that use flour when cooking soups may not be ideal for the Zojirushi Rice Cooker and Warmer because they can expand too much and cause overflow or the lid to burst.

Never keep rice warm for more than 12 hours. Bacteria can form!

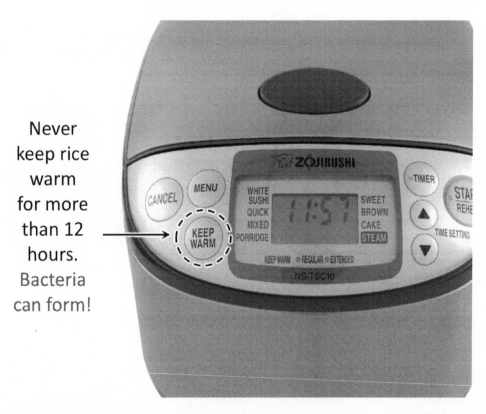

To protect against electrical shock, do not immerse the appliance in water or any other liquid. When cooking with kids, close supervision is necessary. The cord on the Zojirushi Rice Cooker and Warmer is short in length as to keep it away from hot burners or near a heated oven. When cooking your rice or one-pot meals, do not touch, cover or obstruct the steam vent on the top of the rice cooker as it is extremely hot and may burn your skin. Always make sure the outside of the inner pan is dry before use; if the inner pan is returned to the rice cooker wet, it may damage or cause the product to malfunction. Rice should never be left in the inner pan with the KEEP WARM button on for more than 12 hours.

Detailed Process of Using The Zojirushi Rice Cooker

1

Using the provided measuring cup for the type of rice you are cooking, add rice to the inner cup. Rinse and remove excess starch. Place the inner cooking pan into your Zojirushi. Close and secure the lid and plug in the power cord.

2

Select the desired Menu setting by pressing the Menu button. Press the Start/Reheat button.

3

The Start/Reheat light will turn on and you'll hear a beep that means cooking has started. The Display will show the remaining cook time.

4

When finished, you'll hear a beep. The Zojirushi will then switch to Keep Warm. Stir the rice with serving spatula to evenly distribute any remaining moisture.

4

PRO TIPS

Not-In-The-Manual Secrets

When it comes to getting that gorgeous color on your meats and vegetables, you'll want to sear it in a pan after you cook it in the Zojirushi Rice Cooker and Warmer. While the rice cooker takes the long time out of traditional cooking it doesn't have the ability to give your dish or meat that gorgeous, light golden seared color. If you're cooking something like a cheeseburger simply cook in the rice cooker and heat a frying pan on high. Sear on both sides for 1 to 2 minutes, and you've got one quick delicious meal. When it comes to making yogurt, you'll want to place a ceramic bowl into the bottom of the rice cooker. You'll want to heat your milk and use a candy thermometer to measure the temperature. Simply follow the recipe below and you'll come out with perfect, thick yogurt every time. The Zojirushi also gives you the option of choosing a melody or beep sound to alert you when cooking is completed. Simply, put the inner pan in the Zojirushi, plug into a power source, press the Timer Key for more than 3 seconds and the sound changes every time you press this key. Here, you can choose High Melody Sound, Low Melody Sound, or Beep Sound.

Add 1/2 tsp of olive oil

to prevent rice from boiling over.

How to Add Crispiness

When it comes to adding crispness to your meal, you'll want to follow the same rule as searing. Because the rice cooker primarily uses steam and hot water to cook food, you won't be able to crisp chicken. Simply heat a frying pan on high and char for 1 to 2 minutes on each side. Alternatively, you can get that golden brown color in the oven with a broiler. Be sure to heat on high and watch the food as to not burn it! Occasionally, you may need to brush meats with olive oil to crisp. To keep it healthy, measure out 1 tsp. Olive oil and evenly distribute across one serving. You'll only need 1/2 to 1 tsp. per person/per serving.

Secrets to Making Perfect Fluffy Rice Every Time

The secret to making the perfect, fluffy rice every time you cook in your Zojirushi Rice Cooker and Steamer is to use the measuring cup and follow the recipes below. It's that simple. There's no inside tip or trick—just be sure to follow the detailed, yet easy instructions and you'll cook perfect rice in no time—every time! You can also use the rice cooker to flash cook rice in as little as 24 minutes for those really busy days and nights. Just be sure to use the measuring cup that comes with the Zojirushi Rice Cooker and Warmer, and follow the Rice section of the manual included with the appliance. In the event that your rice isn't cooked or hard when the rice cooker switches to KEEP WARM, add 1/2 to 1 cup of water and stir through. Close the lid, lock it in place, and press the RICE switch. When rice cooker switches to KEEP WARM, remove the lid and stir the rice and taste. Repeat as needed until the rice is fluffy and to your desired consistency. If rice is soggy or full of excess water, stir, replace the lid and leave on KEEP WARM for 10 to 30 minutes longer. Stir occasionally to check until cooked through to desired consistency. If your rice keeps turning brown or caramelizing, simply rinse the rice before cooking to avoid this common kitchen mishap.

Best Way to Safely Reheat Rice

You may have read claims that reheated rice can be loaded with bacteria and possibly cause food poisoning. There is a safe way to reheat rice, and we've got the top pro tips for you here! While you might think a microwave is best, the best way is to add 1 tablespoon of water, per bowl of rice or 5.5 ounces, to the rice and reheat it using your Zojirushi Rice Cooker and Warmer. Loosen rice with the spatula and gather rice toward the center of the Inner Pan to avoid scorching or drying out. Set the timer for 5 to 8 minutes and your rice cooker will fluff and rehydrate your rice in no time. Just make sure it's heated through. Make sure the keep-warm lamp is on. Press the cooking/reheat key when the melody sounds and the cooking/reheat lamp will start blinking. If the cooking/reheat key is pressed when the keep-warm lamp is off, the rice cooking function will start – not the reheat. In the event that the rice is not overcooked, just add 2 minutes and check it again. Cook until hot and serve with your favorite vegetables, tofu, chicken, pork, shrimp, or beef.

Seasoning Tips for Yellow and Mexican Rice and Other Specialties

Seasoning rice is a healthy way to make more versatile dishes. Adding broth or stock is a great way to elevate the flavor of your rice like a pro chef. The ratio of broth or stock to the Zojirushi Rice Cooker and Warmer is the same as water to rice ratios on your manual chart or recipe. You can make delicious Yellow Rice for Paella or Spanish themed meals by adding a 1/2 tsp. Turmeric to the rice cooker and substituting chicken or vegetable broth for water. When creating Mexican Rice, do the same by substituting chicken broth for water. Add 1 tsp. Garlic salt, 1/2 tsp. Cumin, 1/2 cup tomato sauce, and 1/4 cup chopped onion. Creating delicious rice dishes in your Zojirushi Rice Cooker and Warmer has never been so easy! You can find more delicious rice recipes to try below.

Extra Tips

If you misplace the measuring cup that comes with your Zojirushi Rice Cooker and Warmer, a 1 standard US cup or 171 ml. is an exact replacement.

When turning the rice cooker off: be sure to press the off button twice and unplug the power cord from the electric outlet. Keep in mind that the function of the steam vent is to help pressure cook and steam your food, so hot steam can escape periodically. Simply keep hands, arms and face away from the steam vent to avoid burning yourself. That means little hands too if you tend to have children in the kitchen.

5

MAIN COURSE RECIPES

Rice Cooker Mahi Mahi

Gorgeous gourmet meals are right at your fingertips when you cook up this delicious mahi-mahi with your Zojirushi Rice Cooker and Warmer. This rice cooker mahi-mahi is absolutely beautiful served on its own, with a side of fresh steamed vegetables, or on a grilled bun as a delightful sandwich.

Serving 4-6
Cooking Time 20 minutes

Ingredients

3 lb. mahi-mahi fish fillets

Coarse sea salt

White Pepper

2 lemons, 1 juiced, 1 cut into wedges

2 tsp. Olive oil

Garnish: lemon wedges and olive oil

Instructions

1. Rinse fish with cold water and pat dry with a paper towel. Rub with olive oil, sea salt, and white pepper.

2. Add 2 cups of water to the inner pan.

3. Place fish in the MIXED key tray and drizzle evenly with lemon juice.

4. Place the MIXED key tray in the rice cooker. Lock lid and MIXED key for 15 minutes or until cooked through; meat should be tender and cooked white through.

5. Transfer onto plates and garnish with additional lemon juice and olive oil.

Nutritional Info: Calories: 218, Sodium: 300 mg, Dietary Fiber: 0.3 g, Fat: 3.8 g, Carbs: 3.1 g, Protein: 42 g.

Massaman Chicken

If you are craving massaman chicken cooked in clay pots from Thailand, this is the recipe for you. Massaman chicken is a delicious one pot meal that can be served light with a side salad and glass of sparkling water for one amazing night in. For a more comforting meal, try serving it with grilled garlic naan bread or basmati rice.

Servings 4
Cook time 1 hour 10 minutes

Ingredients

2/3 cups massaman curry paste

1 cup unsweetened coconut milk, from a can

4 chicken thighs, diced into 1-inch pieces

1/2 cup Belgian wheat beer

1/2 cup low sodium chicken broth

1 cup potato, chopped

1/2 cup onion, chopped

1 tbsp. tamarind paste

1 1/2 tbsp. palm sugar

2-3 bay leaves

1/4 cup roast cardamom

1/4 cup roast peanuts, chopped, for garnish

Instructions

1. Pour the coconut milk and massaman curry paste into the inner pan. Mix them thoroughly and lock the lid in place.

2. Set MIXED key to 15 minutes and start. When cycle is finished, add the rest of the ingredients to the inner pan and stir well to combine.

3. Set MIXED key to 25 minutes for 2 cycles, and an additional 10-minute cycle; total cooking time 1 hour. Chicken should fall apart with the touch of a fork and be very tender.

4. Plate, top with roast peanuts, and enjoy!

Nutritional Info: Calories: 556, Sodium: 931 mg, Dietary Fiber: 16.1 g, Fat: 26.9 g, Carbs: 51 g, Protein: 25.5 g.

Country Style BBQ Ribs

Country style ribs are the perfect dish to prepare for any summer barbecue or backyard picnic. These country style ribs are ready in no time and are just as mouth-watering and delicious as traditional ribs. You can serve them up with a sweet glass of tea or your favorite sides for an amazing meal.

Servings 2
Cooking Time 1 hour 10 minutes

Instructions

1 package Country style ribs, about 5 to 6 ribs

1/3 cup honey

1 tbsp. brown sugar or brown substitute

1 tsp. season salt like Meat Magic Seasoning Salt®

1 (12 oz.) bottle dark beer or stout, like Guinness

1 (16-oz. bottle) barbecue sauce

2 tbsp. olive oil

2 ears of corn, cut in half, husked and rinsed

Instructions

1. Add olive oil to the inner pan of the rice cooker and push the KEEP WARM key.

2. Heat the honey in a microwavable mixing bowl for 15 -25 seconds; add brown sugar and season salt to mixing bowl and combine well. Add ribs and toss to coat well.

3. Add ribs to the rice cooker. Top with the barbecue sauce and very slowly pour beer into the rice cooker to keep from foaming over.

4. Lock lid into place and hit the MIXED key until the rice cooker reads 25 minutes. When the timer goes off, add an additional 25 minutes.

5. Add the corn to the inner pan and place into the rice cooker with the ribs. Lock the lid and select MIXED key for 10 minutes.

6. Let ribs rest for five minutes after rice cooker goes off. Remove corn, then ribs, and plate with your other favorite sides.

Nutritional Info: Calories: 1310, Sodium: 816 mg, Dietary Fiber: 5.8 g, Fat: 42.5 g, Carbs: 176.8 g, Protein: 50 g.

Jambalaya

Serve up some southern charm with this delicious jambalaya recipe. One pot meals are just the thing when it comes to eating in instead of eating out. This jambalaya is so delicious it's sure to knock your socks off!

Servings 5-6
Cook time 50 minutes

Ingredients

1/3 cup onion, diced

1 rib celery, very thinly sliced

1 tsp. olive oil

1/2 lb. andouille sausage, sliced

12 medium shrimp, deveined and peeled (optional)

1/2 cup French onion soup

1/2 cup low sodium chicken stock

2 (10 oz) cans diced tomatoes and green chiles like Rotel drained

1 (15 oz) can black-eyed peas, undrained

11/2 cups white or brown rice, uncooked

Instructions

1. Add olive oil to rice cooker and push KEEP WARM key.

2. Add onion and celery. Push MIXED key to five minutes, lock lid and cook.

3. Open the rice cooker and add remaining ingredients. Stir to combine. Add 25 minutes using the MIXED key on the rice cooker.

4. Once finished, let it sit for 5 minutes; do not remove the lid.

5. Turn the rice cooker to MIXED key for 10 additional minutes.

6. Stir and check rice to make sure it is done. If not, add a little more water (about 2 tbsp), stir, and set it to cook again for an additional five minutes.

7. Serve with your favorite salad or on its own with a light beer or glass of lemonade.

Nutritional Info: Calories: 1417, Sodium: 933 mg, Dietary Fiber: 10.3 g, Fat: 22.8 g, Carbs: 151.1 g, Protein: 143.9 g.

Dijon Chicken with Farro and Mushrooms

One pot meals are a complete highlight to weekly dinner or dinner parties when it comes to using your Zojirushi Rice Cooker and Warmer. This Dijon Chicken is highlighted an elevated with the earthly flavors of farro and mushrooms for one amazing meal. Serve it with a pale ale or glass of sparkling apple juice to really kick things up a notch.

Servings 4

Cook Time 80 minutes

Ingredients

6 boneless chicken thighs, with the fat trimmed off

1 tsp. olive oil

2 shallots, minced

1 cup mushrooms, diced

1 cup farro

1 1/2 cups low-sodium chicken or vegetable broth

Marinade

1 tsp. garlic powder

Pinch of nutmeg

1/3 cup balsamic vinegar

1 tsp. olive oil

1 tbsp. Dijon mustard

Pinch of sea salt

Pinch of ground black pepper

Instructions

1. Add all marinade ingredients to a plastic, resealable bag. Add chicken, turning to make sure each thigh is well-coated with marinade; refrigerate until needed.

2. Add 1 tsp. Olive oil to the inner pan. Add shallots, stirring to coat, then lock lid. Hit the MIXED key once and cook for 5 minutes, until shallots have softened.

3. Open rice cooker and add mushrooms. Hit the MIXED key twice and cook 8 for minutes.

4. Open rice cooker and stir in farro and broth. Place chicken on top of farro mixture; discard any remaining marinade.

5. Lock the lid and select the MIXED key until programmed for 25 minutes. When the program goes offset for an additional 5 minutes.

Check the internal temperature of the chicken with a meat thermometer; if it does not read 165 degrees Fahrenheit - cook for additional 5-minute increments until the ideal temperature is reached.

6. Transfer portions to plates and serve hot with your favorite beverage.

Nutritional Info: Calories: 116, Sodium: 412 mg, Dietary Fiber: 0.9 g, Fat: 4.1 g, Carbs: 9.8 g, Protein: 10.19 g.

Shrimp with Lemon Risotto

The fresh squeezed Taste of lemon really brightens up shrimp and risotto for one delectable meal. The Zojirushi really can help you prepare fancy, restaurant quality meals right in the comfort of your home with ease. You don't have to go all out in order to dine like a king or queen.

Servings 4-6
Cook time 30 minutes

Ingredients

1 tbsp. olive oil

5 tsp. butter

1 cup onion, chopped fine

1/2 cup red bell pepper

1 tbsp. lemon zest

1 cup Arborio rice

1/4 cup white wine, like Sauvignon Blanc

3 cups chicken broth

24 medium shrimp, deveined, peeled and tailed

2 lemons, one juiced, one cut into wedges

1/2 cup parmesan cheese, grated

1/8 tsp. coarse black pepper

1 tbsp. Fresh parsley, chopped

Olive oil for drizzling

Instructions

1. Select the WHITE RICE key. When the bottom of the inner pan gets hot, add olive oil and butter.

2. Add onion and red bell pepper when butter is melted and sauté for about 3 minutes or until softened.

3. Stir in lemon zest.

4. Fold in rice until completely coated. Sauté for about 5 minutes or until mostly translucent.

5. Stir in wine and cook for 3 to 4 minutes or until evaporated. Stir in broth. Close the lid and push the MIXED key to 20 minutes; stir a few times while the risotto is cooking.

6. Fold in shrimp and lemon juice. Set the MIXED key for 5 minutes. Shrimp should be pink and opaque; if risotto is too al dente cook for an additional 5 minutes.

7. Fold in parmesan and black pepper.

8. Serve garnished with parsley, lemon wedges, and an olive oil drizzle on top.

Nutritional Info: Calories: 1496, Sodium: 807 mg, Dietary Fiber: 1.8 g, Fat: 26.4 g, Carbs: 30.1 g, Protein: 283 g.

Ginger Sesame Roasted Pork

Juicy, slow roasted pork is just as easy cooked in your Zojirushi as it is in any traditional method. The best part about any Zojirushi recipe is that you push one button, walk away, and done. Dinner is on the table in no time!

Servings 4-6
Cooking time 30 minutes

Ingredients

1 lb. Pork loin

sea salt

coarse black pepper

1 tsp. sesame oil

3 garlic cloves, chopped

2 tbsp. scallions, thinly sliced

2 tbsp. fresh ginger root, sliced

1 cup soy sauce

2 tsp. sugar or sugar substitute

Instructions

1. Rinse the pork loin and rub generously with sea salt and black pepper.

2. Heat the sesame oil in a non-stick frying pan over medium-high heat. Add the garlic and toast for one minute. Transfer to Zojirushi rice cooker.

3. Add the pork loin to the frying pan and lightly caramelized on both sides; about 3 to 5 minutes each.

4. Transfer the pork to the rice cooker fat side down. Add scallions, ginger, soy sauce, and sugar. Do not fill the rice cooker with liquid over the top liquid lines to avoid overflowing the rice cooker while cooking.

5. Select the WHITE RICE key.

6. Leave the lid on and let pork rest in the rice cooker for five minutes. Remove lid, lift pork out with tongs and cut. If pork is still pink in the center, cook for an additional 10 minutes. Serve with your favorite sides.

Nutritional Info: Calories: 266, Sodium: 926 mg, Dietary Fiber: 0.6 g, Fat: 13.6 g, Carbs: 6.6 g, Protein: 28.2 g.

Balsamic Roast Beef with Rustic Vegetables

Nothing says comfort food on a weekend like rustic roast. This delicious balsamic roast beef with rustic vegetables really hits the spot when it comes to a scrumptious meal. Here, you will learn just how to perfectly braise beef in order to cook the most delicious roast in your Zojirushi.

Serving 6-8
Cook time 1 hour 20 minutes

Ingredients

2 tsp. olive oil, divided

2 1/2 lb. boneless chuck roast

1/2 onion, sliced into 1-inch thick pieces

2 parsnips, diced thick

1 (15 oz) can diced tomatoes

1 cup beef broth

1/2 cup balsamic vinegar

1/2 cup red wine

1 tbsp. Worcestershire sauce

1/2 tsp. Garlic powder

1/2 teaspoon red pepper flakes

4 cloves garlic chopped

Instructions

1. Heat 1 tsp. Olive oil in a large frying pan on high heat. Sear roast beef on each side for 3 minutes and transfer to the rice cooker.

2. Add an additional tablespoon of olive oil to the pan and turn to medium heat. Add onions and saute 3 minutes.

3. Mix balsamic vinegar and wine together in a measuring cup and add to onions to caramelize for 5 minutes.

4. Transfer onions and juice to the rice cooker. Add remaining ingredients and lock the lid in place. Set the MIXED key for a total of 30 minutes. Leave on KEEP WARM for 10 additional minutes.

5. Remove roast from the inner pan, place on a cutting board, and slice. Spoon vegetables and au jus over plated roast to serve.

Nutritional Info: Calories: 531, Sodium: 206 mg, Dietary Fiber: 0.9 g, Fat: 35.2 g, Carbs: 5.5 g, Protein: 40.1 g.

Pad Thai

When you are craving comfort food, this pad thai absolutely hits the spot. Packed with delicious rice noodles, carrots, and bean sprouts - you won't feel like you are dining at home when this savory and sweet, spicy dish hits your taste buds. Garnish with a lime and chopped peanuts for authentic fun!

Serving 4
Cook time 25 minutes

Ingredients

3/4 lbs. chicken, cut into 2-inch strips

8 large shrimp deveined, peeled and tailed

8 oz. Thai Rice Noodles, medium #10

1/4 cup grapeseed oil

3 scallions, topped and thinly sliced

1 medium Carrot shaved into ribbons

1 cup Bean Sprouts

1 1/2 tsp. Fresh garlic, chopped

2 eggs

1 1/2 cups chicken broth

1/2 cup Unsalted Roasted Peanuts crushed, for garnish

1 Lime cut into wedges, for garnish

Pad Thai Sauce

3 tbsp. tamarind paste

1/3 cup light brown sugar or brown sugar substitute

2 tbsp. fish sauce

1 tbsp. fresh lime juice

1 tbsp. tomato paste

1 tsp. ground chili paste, like Sambal Oelek

Instructions

1. Soak Noodles in hot water for 1-2 minutes and drain; noodles should bend slightly.

2. Add Pad Thai Sauce ingredients to a glass mixing bowl and whisk until well-blended.

3. Set selecture cooker to MIXED key for 5 minutes. Add olive oil, garlic, carrots, bean sprouts, and scallions to inner pan. Sauté for 1 minute.

4. Add chicken and sauté 1 minute.

5. Push ingredients to one side of the inner pan and crack eggs into the empty spot and scramble until almost firm. Fold into other ingredients.

6. Add broth. Fold in Pad Thai sauce and stir until well-combined.

7. Gently fold noodles into the sauce.

8. Lock lid in place and set to MIXED key for 5 minutes.

9. Open the lid and lay shrimp on top of the Pad Thai. Replace lid and MIXED key for 5 additional minutes. Place on KEEP WARM for 5 minutes.

10. Plate Pad Thai and serve garnished with peanuts and a lime wedge.

Nutritional Info: Calories: 1389, Sodium: 853 mg, Dietary Fiber: 4.2 g, Fat: 48.2 g, Carbs: 65.4 g, Protein: 180.2 g.

Whole Roasted Chicken

Whole roasted chicken is a delicious way to serve up a family feast, and you don't have to spend all day doing it! When do you whip up this recipe, you can cook a roasted chicken in no time. Serve it with your favorite sides like roasted potatoes, green beans, broccoli casserole, and cranberry sauce - and you'll think it's Thanksgiving.

Serving 6-8
Cook time 1 hour 5 minutes

Ingredients

1 small chicken, up to 2 lbs.

1 tsp. sea salt

1 tsp. black pepper

1 tsp. chili powder

1 tsp. garlic powder

1 lemon

2 tsp. olive oil

2 shallots

1 rib of celery, sliced

Instructions

1. Mix sea salt, black pepper, chili powder, and garlic powder in a small mixing bowl; set aside.

2. Smash the shallots with the flat side of a knife, on a cutting board, to break each into two or three pieces.

3. Cut the lemon into thin slices, then cut slices in half. Slide your fingers under the top skin of the chicken and pull it up, place lemon slices under the skin, and stretch it back over to cover the lemon slices.

4. Heat 1 tsp. olive oil in a frying pan over medium-high heat. Sear the chicken on each side for about 5-8 minutes, or until the skin has darkened and is a little crispy.

5. Rub chicken with the remaining teaspoon of olive oil, and coat oiled chicken with seasoning mix.

6. Shove remaining lemon and shallots into the chicken cavity.

7. Set MIXED key for two full 25-minute rounds and one 20 minute round; total cook time in the rice cooker is one hour.

8.   Chicken is ready to serve when juices run clear, and meat is no longer pink.

Nutritional Info: Calories: 85, Sodium: 273 mg, Dietary Fiber: 0.5 g, Fat: 4 g, Carbs: 1.4 g, Protein: 10.8 g.

Pineapple Chicken Fajitas

When you're craving something a little sweet, pineapple chicken fajitas are just the dish to prepare. You can cook amazing pineapple chicken fajitas that are just as delicious as the ones you get at your local restaurant. When you combine the Savory Spice of chili, cumin, and oregano with sweet pineapple you'll get a tantalizing delicious dish.

Servings 4
Cook time 1 hour 10 minutes

Ingredients

1 lb. chicken thighs

2 bell peppers, any color, sliced thin

1 cup pineapple chunks, drained if using canned

1/2 medium onion, sliced thin

2 cloves garlic

1 tbsp. tomato paste

1 cup chicken broth

1 tsp. chili powder

1 tsp. cumin

1/4 tsp. oregano

1/2 tsp. paprika

1/2 tsp. garlic powder

1/2 teaspoon sea salt

1/4 teaspoon freshly ground black pepper

1 (15 oz.) can black beans, drained

1 tsp. hot sauce

6 corn tortillas

1 avocado, sliced for garnish

1/2 cup sour cream, for garnish

Cotija cheese, for garnish

Instructions

1. Mix the tomato paste, chicken broth, and spices in a small mixing bowl.

2. Add bell peppers, onion, chicken, pineapple, and seasoning mix to inner pan of rice cooker.

3. Close lid and set MIXED key for 40 minutes total. Remove chicken and set aside.

4. Add the black beans and hot sauce. Set MIXED key for an additional 15 minutes, or until the liquid has reduced.

5.   Shred the chicken while the vegetables are cooking. When 15 minutes is up, fold the chicken back into the inner pan of the rice cooker and select KEEP WARM for five minutes to warm the chicken.

6.   Serve on corn tortillas with avocado, sour cream, and cotija cheese.

Nutritional Info: Calories: 815, Sodium: 725 mg, Dietary Fiber: 20.8 g, Fat: 20.3 g, Carbs: 97.7 g, Protein: 63.2 g.

One Pot Teriyaki Chicken and Vegetables

One pot chicken teriyaki and vegetables is the way to go when you were really looking for a quick one pot meal. You can have dinner on the table and 30 minutes or less when you whip out this delicious dish. When you are craving savory meets sweet, with less carbs, this is the meal for you.

Servings 3-4

Cook time 30 minutes

1 1/2 tbsp. sesame oil

1 medium boneless skinless chicken breast, cut into cubes

Sea salt

Black pepper

2 cloves garlic, minced

1/2 tsp. minced ginger

1/3 cup red bell peppers, chopped

1/3 cup carrot, shredded

1 1/2 cups Jasmine rice, rinsed and drained thoroughly

1 cup water

1 cup broccoli florets

1/3 cup frozen shelled Edamame beans, thawed

Sesame seeds, for garnish

Teriyaki Sauce

1/3 cup soy sauce

1/4 cup rice wine vinegar

1/4 cup honey

1 1/2 tbsp. Mirin

1 tsp. cornstarch

3 tbsp. water, plus more as needed to thin out the sauce

Instructions

1. Preheat rice cooker on MIXED key for 5 minutes.

2. Whisk soy sauce, vinegar, honey, mirin and starch in a mixing bowl. Pour into a saucepan and heat on medium high heat. Slowly add water and bring to a boil, until thickened; transfer to a heat-safe bowl.

3. Add sesame oil to inner pan and MIXED key for 1 minute.

4. Add the chicken and season with sea salt and pepper when oil is hot. Saute for 2 minutes, until golden brown.

5. Add the garlic and ginger and cook for another 20 seconds.

6. Fold in 1/2 cup of the teriyaki sauce, rice, bell peppers, carrots, broccoli, edamame, and water; MIXED key for 10 minutes or until vegetables are tender.

7.   Drizzle with additional teriyaki sauce, top with sesame seeds, and serve.

Nutritional Info: Calories: 448, Sodium: 182 mg, Dietary Fiber: 5.5 g, Fat: 8.7 g, Carbs: 60.7 g, Protein: 28.6 g.

Vegetarian Portobello Pot Roast

For the vegetarian at heart, this vegetarian Portobello pot roast is absolutely out of this world. You don't have to be vegan or vegetarian to appreciate this dish either! Hearty and warm, this pot roast is sure to be a fan favorite to cook in your Zojirushi.

Servings 6-8
Cook time 1 hour 10 minutes

Ingredients

1 pound portobello mushrooms, cut into two inch pieces

2 large carrots, peeled and diced

3 large parsnips, diced large

1 rib of celery, chopped

1 cup frozen pearl onions

4 cloves garlic, peeled and minced

3 sprigs fresh thyme

3 cups vegetable stock, divided

1/2 cup dry red wine

3 tbsp. tomato paste

2 tbsp. Vegetarian Worcestershire sauce

2 tbsp. cornstarch

Kosher salt and freshly-cracked black pepper

Egg noodles with butter, optional side

Instructions

1. Add mushrooms, carrots, parsnips, celery, onions, garlic, thyme, 2 1/2 cups vegetable stock, wine and Worcestershire to the inner pan of the rice cooker; gently toss to combine.

2. Lock lid in place and MIXED key for a total of one hour.

3. Whisk together the remaining 1/2 cup vegetable stock and cornstarch until well-combined. Add to the pot roast and gently toss to combine.

4. Continue on MIXED key for an additional 5 minutes, until the sauce thickens.

5. Serve hot and enjoy with buttered egg noodles!

Nutritional Info: Calories: 165, Sodium: 802 mg, Dietary Fiber: 7.5 g, Fat: 0.6 g, Carbs: 32.8 g, Protein: 4.5 g.

Hawaiian Fried Rice

This bright Hawaiian fried rice is a are yummy dish that the whole family will love. When you want to whip up something healthy on a weeknight, Hawaiian fried rice is the way to go. Serve it up with some sparkling water spiked with fresh berries, orange slices, and limes for a fun healthy meal.

Serving 6
Cook time 50 minutes

Ingredients

2 tsp. sesame oil

1/2 tsp. garlic powder

1 small onion, diced

1 red bell pepper, diced

2 cups uncured ham, cooked and diced into 1/2 -inch cubes

3 eggs

1 1/2 cups brown rice, uncooked and rinsed

2 cups water

2 tbsp. soy sauce

1 cup pineapple, diced

1 scallion, sliced thin for garnish

Instructions

1. Add the sesame oil to the inner pan and select MIXED key for five minutes. Heat oil for 2 minutes, then adds the onion and red pepper to saute for remaining 3 minutes. Stir and saute for 5 additional minutes or until softened.

2. Add the ham to the rice cooker and saute for 5 minutes.

3. Beat eggs in a small mixing bowl until well-combined. Push the ham mixture to one side and add the eggs and scramble until firm and cooked through.

4. Add remaining ingredients, stir to combine, lock the lid in place, and set to MIXED key for 25 minutes.

5. Leave Hawaiian Fried Rice on KEEP WARM for 10 minutes. Divide the rice into bowls and garnish with scallions to serve.

Nutritional Info: Calories: 245, Sodium: 704 mg, Dietary Fiber: 2.6 g, Fat: 7.1 g, Carbs: 43.8 g, Protein: 15.9 g.

General Tso's Chicken

If you love General Tso's chicken, you will fall for this recipe fast. General Tso's can be prepared in less time than you can get it from a delivery in your Zojirushi. The best part, is that you can prepare this restaurant quality dish right in the comfort of your kitchen.

Serving 2-4

Cook time 45 minutes

Ingredients

3 garlic cloves, minced

1 tsp. fresh ginger, roughly chopped

1 tbsp. grapeseed oil

10 dried Chinese red chili

5 boneless skinless chicken thighs

1 stalk green onion, green part finely chopped for garnish, white part cut into 1.5-inch pieces

1 tbsp. honey

8-10 pieces of bibb lettuce or romaine

General Tso's Sauce

1/4 cup dark soy sauce

2 tbsp. Shaoxing rice wine

2 tbsp. distilled white vinegar

1/3 cup sugar or sugar substitute

1 tsp. sesame oil

Thickening agent

2 tbsp. cornstarch

2 tbsp. water

Instructions

1. Whisk together the General Tso's Sauce ingredients in a glass mixing bowl until well-combined and set aside.

2. Add grapeseed oil to rice cooker and add 5 minutes to MIXED key. Add garlic and ginger after 2 minutes. Saute until translucent and softened; about 3 minutes.

3. Add dried Chinese red chili, the whites of the green onions. Cook for 3 minutes until fragrant.

4. Add sauce and chicken thighs to the inner pan. Close lid and MIXED key for 25 minutes.

5. Remove the chicken from the inner pan and shred with a fork.

6. Remove the Chinese red chili. Add honey and bring the sauce back to a boil on MIXED key.

7. Mix the cornstarch and water for the thickening agent in a small mixing bowl. Fold into the sauce one third at a time until desired thickness.

8. Fold shredded chicken into the sauce and replace the lid on KEEP WARM for 5 minutes.

9. Assemble lettuce leaves on a plate. Spoon in the desired amount of General Tso's Chicken and garnish with green onion to serve.

Nutritional Info: Calories: 187, Sodium: 103 mg, Dietary Fiber: 0.2 g, Fat: 8 g, Carbs: 6.7 g, Protein: 22.6 g.

Super-Easy Spanish Paella

A traditional Spanish dish, Paella warms the heart and soul. You can fill your belly up on this amazing Spanish dish and feel no guilt whatsoever. Packed with loads of flavor like smoked paprika and saffron, this dish is sure to fast become a favorite of the whole family.

Servings 6

Cook time 40 minutes

Ingredients

2 tbsp. olive oil, divided

1 yellow onion, diced

1 red bell pepper, diced

1 green bell pepper, diced

2 cloves garlic, minced

2 tsp. smoked paprika

2 tsp. dried oregano

1 pinch saffron

3/4 tsp. sea salt

1/2 tsp. crushed red pepper flakes

Coarse ground black pepper

1 bay leaf

1 (15 oz.) can diced tomatoes

3 cups low-sodium vegetable or chicken broth

11/2 cups brown rice

3 boneless skinless chicken thighs, cut into 1-inch pieces

12 large shrimp or tiger prawns, deveined and peeled

1/4 cup chorizo

1/2 cup frozen peas, defrosted

1/4 cup sliced black olives

Hot sauce, for garnish

Freshly chopped parsley, for garnish

Instructions

1. Heat 1 tablespoon olive oil in the rice cooker on MIXED key for 3 minutes.

2. Add onion and bell peppers. Cook until soft, about 7 minutes.

3. Add garlic to rice cooker and sauté for 1 minute or until fragrant.

4. Add the broth, then fold in smoked paprika, oregano, sea salt, crushed red pepper, black pepper, bay leaf, diced tomatoes with liquid, and rice. Select BROWN RICE key and cook through the cycle.

5. Heat remaining olive oil in a frying pan over medium-high heat. Add chicken thighs and chorizo. Cook until browned and no pink shows in the chicken; about 10 to 12 minutes. Fold cooked chicken and sausage into the rice.

6. Add saffron, peas, and black olives to the rice cooker.

7. MIXED key for 5 minutes to combine flavors.

8. Serve garnished with hot sauce and chopped parsley.

Nutritional Info: Calories: 844, Sodium: 844 mg, Dietary Fiber: 9.3 g, Fat: 16.1 g, Carbs: 144 g, Protein: 36 g.

Honey Bourbon Chicken

Glaze your chicken with a taste of the South when you cook up this delicious honey bourbon chicken in your Zojirushi. Why not try something different when it comes to tailgates and weekend BBQs? Honey Bourbon Chicken is just the way to go when it comes to a new recipe that everyone will start asking you to share.

Servings 4
Cook Time 20 minutes

Ingredients

4-5 boneless skinless chicken thighs

1/2 tsp. garlic powder

2 tsp. ground chili paste, like Sambal Oelek

3/4 cups ketchup

3/4 cups honey

1/4 cup bourbon, like Maker's Mark

2 tbsp. potato starch

1 bag frozen broccoli, thawed

Instructions

1. Add water, ketchup, honey, bourbon, chili paste, and garlic to the inner pan and stir to combine.

2. Fold in chicken and coat well.

3. Lock lid and select MIXED key for 10 minutes.

4. Remove some sauce and transfer to a glass measuring cup. Whisk in potato starch until dissolved. Fold into the inner pan with chicken.

5. Place broccoli in the MIXED key tray and place in the rice cooker. Replace lid and MIXED key for an additional 10 minutes.

6. Plate together and enjoy!

Nutritional Info: Calories: 816, Sodium: 974 mg, Dietary Fiber: 1.5 g, Fat: 18.3 g, Carbs: 69.5 g, Protein: 90.3 g.

6

RICE RECIPES (WHITE/BROWN/BASMATI/MULTI-GRAIN...ETC.)

The Perfect Sushi Rice

Sushi rice has never been so easy when it comes to the Zojirushi. The Zojirushi was created to help you cook meals in no time, and this is just the recipe when you are craving fresh, delicious food. With this amazing rice cooker and warmer you'll get the most perfect sushi rice every time.

Servings 8
Cook time 30 minutes

Ingredients

4 cups short grain/sushi rice

Water

Su for Sushi Rice

1 cup rice wine vinegar

1/2 cup sugar

1/4 cup mirin

Instructions

1. Add rice to the inner pan. Fill with water to line 4. Set FLASH RICE to 27 minutes.

2. Heat vinegar, sugar, and mirin in a saucepan until sugar is dissolved; let cool to room temperature.

3. Gently fold the Su into the rice.

4. Let rice stand for 10 minutes and fold again.

5. Use the sushi rice to create your favorite sushi or host a sushi building party!

Nutritional Info: Calories: 213, Sodium: 66 mg, Dietary Fiber: 0 g, Fat: 0.2 g, Carbs: 45.5 g, Protein: 2.4 g.

Rice Cooker Pasta

You don't have to go all out when it comes to your one pot meals. If you are craving scrumptious pasta, this recipe is for you. Top it with your favorite sauces or leave it plain with simple olive oil and sea salt for a delicious one meal dish.

Servings 3
Cook time 25 minutes

Ingredients

2 cups uncooked pasta

2 cups water

1/4 tsp. sea salt

1 tsp. olive oil

1 cup favorite sauce, or 4 tsp.
Butter, optional

1/2 tsp. garlic powder,
optional

parmesan cheese, for topping

Instructions

1. Place water, pasta, sea salt and olive oil in the inner pan of the rice cooker, and gently stir to combine. Here, you can also add your favorite sauce or butter, and garlic powder.

2. Close lid and select FLASH RICE; stir once or twice during the cycle to keep from sticking together.

3. Do not leave on warm to keep from browning or caking together. You can pan fry meat like ground round or chicken to add in at the beginning of the cooking process.

4. Serve with your favorite sauce, veggies, meat, or enjoy on its own with butter and cheese!

Nutritional Info: Calories: 359, Sodium: 271 mg, Dietary Fiber: 0.1 g, Fat: 13.2 g,
Carbs: 47.4 g, Protein: 12.8 g.

Spanish Rice

The perfect side to any Mexican meal is none other than Spanish rice. This recipe will help you whip up some delicious Spanish rice in no time. Enjoy it with your favorite Mexican dishes, fill a Southwest burrito with your Spanish rice, or simply eat it on its own with steamed vegetables for a delicious meal.

Servings 4-5
Cook time 35 minutes

Ingredients

2 cups rice

1 tsp. olive oil

1 (14 oz.) can diced tomatoes

3 1/2 cups water

1 small yellow onion, diced

3 chicken or vegetable bouillon cubes

2 tbsp. chili powder

1 tsp. cumin

1/2 tsp. sea salt

1/2 tsp. garlic powder

Instructions

1. Combine rice, water, and diced tomatoes in the inner pan.

2. Fold in the onion, bouillon cubes and spices into the rice and stir well to help the spices dissolve in the water.

3. Select the WHITE RICE key.

4. Keep warm until serving with your favorite lean meats, enchiladas, or tacos! Alternatively, you can use the rice to fill burritos for an authentic South Western meal.

Nutritional Info: Calories: 437, Sodium: 284 mg, Dietary Fiber: 3.3 g, Fat: 4.7 g, Carbs: 65.6 g, Protein: 31 g.

Basmati Rice

Delicious and fluffy, basmati rice is often overlooked because of how much time it takes to cook. You can cut the traditional cooking time when you fix basmati rice right in your Zojirushi. You can also easily warm up rice in your Zojirushi to help you create amazing leftover meals that you have prepped in your rice cooker and warmer.

Servings 4
Cook time 40 minutes

Ingredients

2 cups Basmati Rice

Water

Pinch of sea salt

1 tsp. olive oil

Cardamom pods, optional

Bay leaf, optional

Instructions

1. Add rice to a large mixing bowl. Cover with water and let soak for 30 minutes.

2. Drain rice and rinse, with tap water, until water runs clear.

3. Rinse the rice. Run tap water in the bowl.

4. Pour rice into rice cooker and add 1 cup of water per 1 cup of rice.

5. Add sea salt and olive oil, as well as optional seasonings like Cardamom or Bay Leaf.

6. Lock lid in place, select the WHITE RICE key; when cooking cycle stops, leave on KEEP WARM for 10 minutes and serve!

Nutritional Info: Calories: 353, Sodium: 63 mg, Dietary Fiber: 1.7 g, Fat: 1.9 g, Carbs: 75.1 g, Protein: 6.8 g.

Multigrain Rice

Multigrain Rice isn't usually the first rice you want to cook because of the lengthy cooking times. With your Zojirushi Rice Cooker and Warmer you can cook healthy multi-grain rice with the click of a button. What does Zojirushi, you can explore loads of tantalizing, healthy cooking options now that you can cut the time in half.

Servings 8
Cook time 45-55 minutes

Ingredients

2 cups white rice

4 cups water

1 - 2 cups of any grain on the list below. (Keep in mind: your rice cooker only holds 4 cups of grains, so do not overfill.)

Brown rice, Sweet brown rice, White rice, Wild rice, Red rice, Pearl barley, Steel cut oats, Amaranth, Sorghum, Millet, Black rice, Farro, Buckwheat, Quinoa, Black-eye peas, Soy Beans, Split peas, Garbanzo beans, Kidney beans, Mung beans, Sesame seeds

Instructions

1. Combine your choice of grains and white rice in a large mixing bowl. Gently rinse the rice mixture twice in cold water; drain the water as much as possible without losing the grains in the sink.

2. Add the multigrain rice to the rice cooker and fill with 4 cups of water or to the FILL LINE 4. Select the BROWN RICE key.

3. KEEP WARM for 10 minutes, fluff multigrain rice and serve. You can store the leftover rice in a freezer bag for future use; to thaw, microwave your desired amount on high for 2-3 minutes.

Nutritional Info: Calories: 1143, Sodium: 33 mg, Dietary Fiber: 30.7 g, Fat: 21.2 g, Carbs: 194.1 g, Protein: 46.8 g.

Brown Rice

The clean eating phenomenon has really pushed brown rice to be a star dish. This amazing recipe will help you whip up fluffy, brown rice in less than the regular cooking time. When you are looking to add whole grains to your diet this brown rice recipe will help you do that in less time.

Servings 2
Cook time 40 minutes

Ingredients

1 cup brown rice   *Water*

Instructions

1.   Add brown rice to the inner pan of rice cooker.

2.   Add water to FILL LINE 1.

3.   Stir, lock lid in place, and select the BROWN RICE key.

4.   You can adjust the recipe to make more servings by following this simple rule: For every cup of rice, add water to the corresponding fill line: 1 cup, line 1; 2 cups, line 2, and so on.

5.   Fluff with a fork and serve with your favorite meals!

Nutritional Info: Calories: 344, Sodium: 4 mg, Dietary Fiber: 3.2 g, Fat: 2.6 g, Carbs: 72.4 g, Protein: 7 g.

Cauliflower Rice

The mother of all additions to clean eating is none other than cauliflower rice! Cauliflower rice is an absolute star when used in substitution for whole grain rice. You might not be gluten-free, and just feel like you need to cut some grains from your life, cauliflower rice makes it simple because it takes on so many yummy flavors from Asian to Italian.

Servings 4
Cook time 25 minutes

Ingredients

1 head of cauliflower

2 tsp. olive oil

1/4 tsp. sea salt

1/8 tsp. white pepper

Instructions

1. Rinse the cauliflower and trim off the leaves. Cut cauliflower into 5 to 7 large pieces.

2. Add 1 cup of water to the inner pan, then add cauliflower.

3. Lock the lid and set MIXED key for 5 minutes.

4. Remove the cauliflower to a cutting board.

5. Discard the water in the rice cooker.

6. Add the olive oil to the inner pan and cooked cauliflower.

7. Break up with a potato masher or wooden spoon.

8. Add sea salt and white pepper; stir to combine well.

9. Replace lid, lock, and set to MIXED key for 20 minutes.

10. Enjoy with your favorite dishes for a grain-free alternative. Alternatively, for an Asian inspired meal - swap the olive oil for sesame oil.

Nutritional Info: Calories: 40, Sodium: 137 mg, Dietary Fiber: 1.9 g, Fat: 2.4 g, Carbs: 4.3 g, Protein: 1.4 g.

Vegetable Rice

Vegetarian and vegan dishes are just as easy to whip up in your Zojirushi. You will absolutely fall head over heels for this delicious savory dish. You don't have to be vegetarian or vegan to appreciate just how delicious this vegetable rice truly is!

Servings 4
Cook time 30 minutes

Ingredients

2 cups Jasmine rice

1 small carrot, finely chopped

1/4 cup white cabbage, shredded

1/2 small onion, finely chopped

1/3 cup green beans, chopped small

8 key mushrooms, chopped small

3 tbsp. soy sauce, extra for drizzling

2 tbsp. sake

1 1/2 tbsp. mirin

1/2 tsp. sea salt

3 scallions, finely chopped

Instructions

1. Add rice to the rice cooker inner pan and rinse until water runs clear; drain.

2. Place inner pan in the rice cooker. Add soy sauce, sake, mirin, and salt and add water up to the FILL LINE 2, measuring line, in the pot.

3. Top with carrots, cabbage, onion, green beans, and mushrooms; do not stir.

4. Lock the lid in place and set the rice cooker to WHITE RICE.

5. Gently fluff the rice with a fork and serve hot topped with scallions and extra soy sauce!

Nutritional Info: Calories: 399, Sodium: 980 mg, Dietary Fiber: 6.7 g, Fat: 0.4 g, Carbs: 84.6 g, Protein: 11.8 g.

No Fuss Beans

Beans are delicious powerhouse of protein, complex carbs and fibers all-in-one amazing dish. Gone are the days of waiting hours to cook up a pot of beans. You can cook no-fuss beans in no time when you use your Zojirushi.

Servings 3
Cook time 25 hours 30 minutes

Ingredients

2 cup dried beans, like pinto, navy or black beans

1 bay leaf

1 small ham hock, optional (for vegetarian add 1 vegetable bouillon cube)

Water

Chopped onion, optional

Black pepper, optional

Sea salt, optional

Instructions

1.   Add beans to the inner pan and cover with water; soak overnight.

2.   Drain and rinse the beans, the following morning, put them back in the rice cooker, and add 4 cups of water, along with 1 bay leaf and a ham hock or bouillon cube.

3.   Turn the rice cooker to WHITE RICE and cook for one hour.

4.   Check that beans are still covered with water after the cycle; if needed, add a little more water and set WHITE RICE cycle for the second time.

5.   Remove the bay leaf and ham hock. Serve beans hot as a soup with chopped onion, sea salt, and pepper - or drain and use in your favorite recipes.

Nutritional Info: Calories: 570, Sodium: 192 mg, Dietary Fiber: 20.5 g, Fat: 8.3 g, Carbs: 84.2 g, Protein: 41.4 g.

Quick and Easy Lentils

Low-fat, lean protein options are easy when you use your rice cooker and warmer. Quick and easy lentils are great way to add protein to salads, soups, and even as a substitute for rice or risotto. Quick and easy lentils are also vegetarian and vegan for those that live a more sustainable lifestyle.

Servings: 1-2
Cook time 1 hour 10 minutes

Ingredients

1 cup lentils

Water

1 tbsp. olive oil

1/4 tsp. sea salt

1/8 tsp. coarse black pepper

Instructions

1. Pour lentils into a colander and rinse with cold water.

2. Add the lentils to the rice cooker, top with 2 cups of water; stir to combine.

3. Fold in olive oil, sea salt, and black pepper.

4. Lock lid into place, select BROWN RICE, and cook one hour. Leave on KEEP WARM for 10 minutes after the cycle is finished.

5. Transfer the lentils to a bowl and serve.

Nutritional Info: Calories: 400, Sodium: 6 mg, Dietary Fiber: 29.4 g, Fat: 8.3 g, Carbs: 8 g, Protein: 24.8 g.

7

VEGETABLE AND SIDE DISH
RECIPES

Steamed Broccoli

A quick snack, a side dish, or even just a veggie that really elevates your meal - broccoli can be a real star of your diet when it is steamed. Broccoli is also a great source of vitamin C and K, so you will love the added benefits of this delicious dish. You can even refrigerate steamed broccoli and add it to your morning smoothie for a boost of fiber!

Servings: 4-6

Cook time 5 minutes

Ingredients

1 head of broccoli

2 cups of water

Sea salt, garnish

Lemon wedges, garnish

Olive oil, optional garnish

Instructions

1. Cut the florets off the broccoli and discard the stalk (or reserve for another use).

2. Pour 2 cups of water into rice cooker pot.

3. Rinse florets in running water and place in inner pan. Place basket in the rice cooker and close lid.

4. Using the MIXED key COOK feature, MIXED key broccoli for 3 minutes; don't leave on keep warm or broccoli will wilt.

5. Remove broccoli, plate with your favorite meal. Garnish with sea salt, lemon juice and a drizzle of olive oil.

Nutritional Info: Calories: 51, Sodium: 171 mg, Dietary Fiber: 0.9 g, Fat: 4.8 g, Carbs: 2.2 g, Protein: 0.9 g.

Cuban Black Beans and Rice

Cuban black beans and rice are delicious way to pack more fiber in your diet. This healthy, delicious dish can be served on its own, with a side of grilled pita bread, or with rice for a one dish meal. Cuban black beans are also great to use as a base for dips, to add to salsa, or even burritos for some spicy fun!

Servings 4-6
Cook time 1 hour 10 minutes

Ingredients

2 cups black beans, dry

4 cups water

1 small onion, chopped

1 small green bell pepper, chopped

1 clove garlic, minced

1 tsp. olive oil

1 tsp. cumin

1/4 tsp. oregano

1/4 tsp. garlic powder

1/4 tsp. sugar or sugar substitute

1 bay leaf

1/3 cup white wine

Olive oil, for garnish

Instructions

1.   Add black beans to the inner pan and cover with water; soak overnight.

2.   Drain and rinse the beans, the next morning put them back in the rice cooker, and add 4 cups of water, along with 1 bay leaf.

3.   Turn the rice cooker to WHITE RICE and cook for 30 minutes.

4.   Add one teaspoon of olive oil to a frying pan. Add onion and green pepper. Cook until translucent; about 5-7 minutes. Add garlic and cook for 1 minute longer.

5.   After beans are finished cooking, fold in the onion mixture, seasoning, sugar, and white wine.

6.   Add WHITE RICE cycle for the second time.

7.   Serve beans hot over white rice and enjoy!

Nutritional Info: Calories: 273, Sodium: 10mg, Dietary Fiber: 10.5 g, Fat: 1.9 g, Carbs: 44 g, Protein: 14.4 g.

Rice Cooker Bread

Homemade bread warms the heart and belly. If you are living the lifestyle in which you were concerned about all the preservatives and additives in our daily meals, this recipe will knock your socks off! This Rice Cooker Bread will really transform the way you eat your soups, sandwiches, and breakfast toast!

Servings 8-10

Cook time 29 hours

Ingredients

3 cups all-purpose or bread flour, additional flour for dusting

1/4 tsp. instant yeast

1 1/4 tsp. salt

1 1/2 cups water

Instructions

1. Combine the dry ingredients in the rice cooker and fold in 11/2 cups of water until well-combined.

2. Leave the dough to rise in an unplugged rice cooker 12-18 hours; do not let rise for more than 18 hours as the dough will break down and not bake. You will know it is ready when the bubbles appear on the surface.

3. Dust the top of the dough with flour, then flour your hands. Fold the dough over onto itself twice. Use your hands to tuck the dough under itself to form a round loaf.

4. Leave to rise for an additional 2 hours. Select the WHITE RICE key.

5. Gently lift the bread up flip it over. Select the WHITE RICE key; flip for a second time on each side for a total cook time of 2 hours.

6. Bread is ready when slightly golden on both sides. You can brown the crust even further by finishing the loaf in the oven at 450 degrees Fahrenheit for 10-15 minutes.

Nutritional Info: Calories: 137, Sodium: 291mg, Dietary Fiber: 1 g, Fat: 0.4 g, Carbs: 28.7 g, Protein: 3.9 g.

Quinoa and Pomegranate Salad

Sweet and sour meets savory for one bright salad with this scrumptious recipe! If you love the tart flavor of pomegranate and the earthy flavors of quinoa, you will really want to try this recipe. Serve it with a side of pita bread and hummus, sparkling water, or your favorite protein for one delicious meal.

Servings: 2
Cook time 20 minutes

Ingredients

2 cups quinoa, rinsed

4 cups water

pinch of sea salt

1/2 lemon, juiced

2 tsp. olive oil

1/8 tsp. Coarse ground black pepper

1 tsp. honey

1 tsp. balsamic vinegar

1 cup pomegranate seeds

1/2 cup chopped fresh mint

Manchego cheese, chopped, optional garnish

Instructions

1. Add quinoa, water, and a pinch of salt to the Zojirushi Rice Cooker and Warmer. Lock lid in place and select WHITE RICE.

2. Open the lid and transfer quinoa to a large mixing bowl.

3. Add everything except mint and cheese; stir well to combine.

4. Gently fold in mint and cheese and enjoy!

Nutritional Info: Calories: 247, Sodium: 49mg, Dietary Fiber: 4.7 g, Fat: 5.1 g, Carbs: 42.4 g, Protein: 8.5 g.

Cheesy Jalapeno Bread

Cheesy jalapeno bread will soon become a family favorite when it comes to snacks, tailgate food, and even just something to whip up on the weekend. Ooey gooey cheese meets spicy jalapenos for a taste explosion! This is some seriously delicious bread that you can cook right in your rice cooker.

Servings 4-6
Cook time 2 hours 45 minutes

Ingredients

2 1/2 cups bread flour

1 tsp. yeast

1 1/2 tbsp. sugar, plus one pinch

1 1/2 tsp. salt

1 1/2 tbsp. butter

2 tbsp. milk

3/4 cups water

3/4 cups pickled jalapenos, chopped

1/2 cup white cheddar cheese, shredded

Instructions

1. Add yeast to a large mixing bowl. Fold in a pinch of sugar and about 1/4 cup warm water; set aside for 10 minutes while yeast activates. When activated yeast will look foamy.

2. Add flour, salt, and sugar into the inner pan of the rice cooker and stir to combine.

3. Fold the milk and then the yeast into inner pan. Use hands to mix and form a dough ball.

4. Stick the butter in the middle of the dough ball. Add jalapenos and knead for 10 minutes until butter and jalapenos are incorporated.

5. Form the dough back into a ball and place in the inner pan of the rice cooker to rise for 30 minutes, if it rises too much it will stick to the top of the rice cooker. When the dough has risen, use your hand to form it into a ball again, then let it rise for an additional hour.

6. Select WHITE RICE and cook for one hour. After one hour, flip the bread, sprinkle with cheddar cheese and cook for an additional 45 minutes to 1 hour.

Nutritional Info: Calories: 272, Sodium: 745mg, Dietary Fiber: 1.6 g, Fat: 6.9 g, Carbs: 43.5 g, Protein: 8.2 g.

Mediterranean Quinoa Salad with Red Wine Vinaigrette

Did you know that you can whip up delicious salads with your Sochi Russia? Enjoy summer or spring even more, anytime of the year, with this delicious, bright dish. Mediterranean quinoa meats sweet, tart red wine vinaigrette for a delicious lunch or dinner side dish option.

Servings 6
Cook time 40 minutes

Ingredients

1/2 cup quinoa

2/3 cups water

1/2 cups onion, chopped

1/2 cups cucumbers, diced

1/2 cups black cherries, diced

1/2 cups cherry tomatoes, chopped

1/2 cup buffalo mozzarella, coarsely chopped

For the vinaigrette:

2 tbsp. olive oil

1 tbsp. red wine, like Chianti

1 tbsp. balsamic vinegar

1/2 tsp. garlic powder

1/8 tsp. sugar or sugar substitute

1 dash sea salt, to taste

Instructions

1. Rinse quinoa under cold running water for a few seconds, until water runs clear.

2. Add quinoa and water to the inner pan rice cooker and select FLASH RICE.

3. Add vinaigrette ingredients to a small mixing bowl and whisk until well-combined.

4. Fluff the quinoa with a fork and transfer to a large mixing bowl; let cool for about 5 minutes.

5. Fold in the vegetables and cheese.

6. Pour the red wine vinaigrette over the salad and toss to serve.

Nutritional Info: Calories: 67, Sodium: 24mg, Dietary Fiber: 1.4 g, Fat: 1.3 g, Carbs: 11 g, Protein: 3.1g.

Cheesy Polenta

Polenta is an absolute winner when it comes to Preparing foods for those on a gluten-free diet. Of course, you don't have to be gluten-free in order to enjoy this delicious recipe. This low carbohydrate food is packed with vitamin A and C and is best served as a side to your main meal or topped with fresh grilled veggies like summer squash, zucchini, and bell peppers.

Servings 4
Cook time 40 minutes

Ingredients

2 tbsp. butter

1/2 sweet onion, chopped

1 shallot, minced

1 cup chicken broth

1 cup milk

1/2 cup polenta

1/4 tsp. sea salt, or more to taste

1/4 cup mozzarella cheese, shredded

1/4 cup parmesan cheese, shaved

Instructions

1. Add butter, onion, and shallot to rice cooker inner pan; lock the lid in place and cook on WHITE RICE until onion is soft and translucent, stirring occasionally 10 to 15 minutes.

2. Add chicken broth, milk, polenta, and sea salt. Replace lid and cook on WHITE RICE, for 20 minutes until polenta has absorbed the liquid; stir occasionally.

3. Fold in the cheese and stir until melted. Serve hot and enjoy!

Nutritional Info: Calories: 178, Sodium: 361mg, Dietary Fiber: 0.8 g, Fat: 9.3 g, Carbs: 20.5 g, Protein: 7.7 g.

Steamed Artichokes

Delicious steamed artichokes are right at your fingertips with this wonderful recipe. Artichokes are beautiful on their own when seasoned with simple olive oil, lemon, and sea salt. Of course, you can even chop these delicious artichokes up and throw them in your favorite soups, salads, and pastas for even more tantalizing, versatile dishes.

Serving 2
Cook Time 30 minutes

Ingredients

2 whole artichokes

2 lemons, cut into wedges

olive oil, for drizzling

sea salt, to serve

Instructions

1. Cut a third of the top off of an artichoke. Trim the stem off as well as any thorny tips from the outer leaves.

2. Rub lemon wedges over the cut edges to prevent browning.

3. Add 3/4 cups of water to the inner pan of the rice cooker.

4. Add the artichoke to the inner pan, place in MIXED keyer, lock lid into place. MIXED key for 20 to 30 minutes, or until leaves pull off easily.

5. Remove from rice MIXED keyer, drizzle with olive oil and a dash of sea salt to serve.

Nutritional Info: Calories: 137, Sodium: 355mg, Dietary Fiber: 8.6 g, Fat: 7.1 g, Carbs: 18.4 g, Protein: 4.6g.

Garlic Mashed Potatoes

Creamy, smooth garlic mashed potatoes are a cinch in your rice cooker and warmer. This delicious dish is best served alongside a marbled steak, grilled salmon, or grilled tofu. You can also easily reheat your garlic mashed potatoes using the warmer option in your Zojirushi.

Serving 4-6
Cooking Time 25 minutes

Ingredients

1 pound russet potatoes, peeled and cut into 2-inch chunks

2 garlic cloves, peeled and cut in half

1 cup sour cream

1 stick of butter, salted

1 tsp. sea salt

1 tsp. black pepper

1/2 cup milk

Instructions

1. Add 3 cups of water to the inner pan place the potatoes and garlic in the inner pan in the rice cooker.

2. Press MIXED key for 25 minutes; cook until very tender.

3. Meanwhile, combine the cream, 3/4 cup (1 1/2 sticks) of the butter; and the salt in a medium saucepan and heat until the cream simmers and the butter melts. When the potatoes are tender, put them through a ricer or the medium blade of a food mill.

4. Transfer potatoes and garlic to a large mixing bowl. Add butter, sour cream, salt, pepper, and half the milk. Mash until butter starts to dissolve.

5. Add the other half of the milk and continue to mash until smooth. If potatoes are still lumpy add an additional tablespoon of sour cream until they blend smooth.

6. Return to the rice cooker inner pan and KEEP WARM until ready to serve.

Nutritional Info: Calories: 282, Sodium: 455mg, Dietary Fiber: 1.9 g, Fat: 23.8 g, Carbs: 15.1 g, Protein: 3.4 g.

Hummus

Hummus is a delicious, healthy dip you can whip up to help you eat more veggies. Enjoy it with carrot and celery sticks, cucumber slices, broccoli, cauliflower, and even turnip slices. Dress sandwiches and wraps, or even put a dollop on your full breakfast toast! No matter how you fix it, you'll love this hummus.

Servings 2-4
Cook time 20 minutes

Ingredients

1 cup dry chickpeas, soaked

1 bay leaf

3 garlic cloves, crushed

3 tbsp. tahini

1 lemon, juiced

1/4 tsp. powdered cumin

1/2 tsp. sea salt

Paprika, to serve

Extra virgin olive oil, to serve

Instructions

1. Rinse the chickpeas and add to the inner pan of the rice cooker. Add two crushed garlic cloves and the Bay Leaf. Close and lock the lid and select WHITE RICE to 18 minutes.

2. Drain the chickpeas, reserving all of the cooking liquid. Discard the bay leaf and set aside to cool.

3. Add chickpeas to a food processor or mash with a potato masher.

4. Fold one 1/2 cup of cooking liquid into the mash with the tahini, lemon juice, cumin and 1 fresh garlic clove (depending on your preference). Puree mix until creamy; if not at desired creaminess, fold in extra cooking liquid.

5. Dust with sea salt and paprika. Drizzle with olive oil. Enjoy alongside your favorite pita bread or veggie sticks.

Nutritional Info: Calories: 258, Sodium: 260mg, Dietary Fiber: 10.1 g, Fat: 12.7 g, Carbs: 35 g, Protein: 11.9 g.

Sweet Potatoes

A great side dish alternative to mashed potatoes - sweet potatoes! These delicious delicacies are best served with duck breast, tuna steaks, or on sweet salads. You can also mash them the same way you would white potatoes and enjoy them with a yummy Sunday roast.

Servings 4-6
Cook time 40 minutes

Ingredients

4 sweet potatoes, cut in half

2 cups water

Butter, for garnish

Cinnamon, for garnish

Sea salt, for garnish

Black pepper, for garnish

Instructions

1. Add 2 cups of water to the inner pan.
2. Add sweet potatoes to the inner pan, and place inside the rice cooker.
3. Lock lid in place and set to MIXED key for 35 minutes.
4. Garnish with butter, cinnamon, sea salt and black pepper.

Nutritional Info: Calories: 75, Sodium: 90mg, Dietary Fiber: 2.6 g, Fat: 0.1 g, Carbs: 17.5 g, Protein: 1.4 g.

Potato Salad

Whip up this all American dish for endless foodie fun right in the comfort of your kitchen. Creamy potato salad is the perfect complement to any barbecue or grilled meat with a glass of sweet tea or lemonade. You also love this dish as a lunch side portion or even one bowl meal!

Servings 4-6
Cook time 35 minutes

Ingredients

6 russet potatoes, peeled and cubed

1 1/2 cups water

3 eggs

1/4 cup sweet onion, chopped

1 cup red bell pepper, diced

1 cup sour cream

1/4 cup mayonnaise

1 tsp. yellow mustard

1/8 tsp. Worcestershire sauce

1/8 tsp. Sugar or sugar substitute

2 tbsp finely chopped celery

1 tbsp. dill pickle juice

Sea salt, for serving

Black pepper, for serving

Instructions

1. Add the water to the inner pan. Add potatoes and the eggs to the inner pan. Lock the lid in place and set MIXED key for 35 minutes; remove eggs at 25 minutes and place them in an ice bath to cool.

2. Return potatoes to MIXED key for another 10 to 15 minutes or until tender, but not falling apart.

3. Combine onion, bell pepper, sour cream, mayo, yellow mustard, Worcestershire sauce, sugar, and pickle juice in a large mixing bowl.

4. Gently fold potatoes into the sour cream mixture.

5. Peel and chop the cooled eggs. Gently fold them into the potato salad.

6. Add sea salt and black pepper to taste.

7. Place in the refrigerator and chill at least one hour before serving.

Nutritional Info: Calories: 312, Sodium: 509mg, Dietary Fiber: 5.6 g, Fat: 13.8 g, Carbs: 40.7 g, Protein: 8 g.

8

BREAKFAST RECIPES

Old Fashioned Oatmeal

Creamy, comforting oats are delicious way to start the day. You can dress up your old fashioned oatmeal with anything from honey to Cinnamon, as well as your favorite fruits. Well old fashioned oats can be a star dish, there are also great served with boiled eggs and yogurt.

Servings 1
Cook time 21 minutes

Ingredients

1/2 cup rolled oats

1 cup water

1 pinch of sea salt

Milk or almond milk, for serving

Honey, for serving

Cinnamon, for serving

Instructions

1. Add all of the ingredients to the inner pan of the rice cooker.

2. Select the WHITE RICE key and allow to cook until timer beeps.

3. Open the lid and stir the oats.

4. Fold in milk, honey, and cinnamon, if desired, and serve while hot.

Nutritional Info: Calories: 341, Sodium: 360mg, Dietary Fiber: 7.8 g, Fat: 7.8 g, Carbs: 62.5 g, Protein: 13.7 g.

Vanilla Yogurt Parfait

Vanilla yogurt parfait is just as easy and quick to make in a rice cooker and warmer than it is on a stove-top method. You will love how easy it is to create creamy vanilla yogurt and top with your favorite granola, honey, or fruit for a delicious snack or meal.

Servings 1
Cook time 16 hours 15 minutes

Ingredients

4 1/4 cups milk

1/2 cup yogurt

1 tsp. pure vanilla extract

1 whole nectarine, sliced, for garnish

1/4 cup granola, for garnish

1 tsp. Honey, for garnish

Instructions

1. Add milk to inner pan of rice cooker and heat milk on MIXED key for 2 to 3 hours; until the candy thermometer reads 181 degrees Fahrenheit.

2. Fill a large container with ice and water. Place the inner pan of milk in to cool to 110 degrees Fahrenheit; be careful not to submerge it or get any water in the milk.

3. Remove one cup of the warm milk. Fold in the 1/2 cup of yogurt using a whisk. Next, whisk the mixture into the milk in the inner pan.

4. Place the inner pan of inoculated milk into the rice cooker, cover with a thick kitchen towel for 8 hours.

5. Fold in the vanilla extract in gently until well-combined. Transfer the inner pan to the refrigerator to chill for 8 hours.

6. Once the yogurt is set, top yogurt with nectarines, honey, and granola to complete your breakfast parfait. Additionally, you can top yogurt with chocolate chunks, sliced bananas, and granola for a more decadent breakfast.

Nutritional Info: Calories: 709, Sodium: 590mg, Dietary Fiber: 7.5 g, Fat: 37.9 g, Carbs: 114.6g, Protein: 51.1 g.

Giant Rice Cooker Pancake with Maple Syrup and Berry Compote

For the pancake lever at heart, we even created a delectable giant pancake recipe just for you! Top it with your favorite pancake toppings. Stuff it with your favorites like bananas, blueberries, or chocolate chips. No matter how you love your pancakes - this recipes is one sweet treat!

Servings 2-4
Cook time 50 minutes

Ingredients

2 cups unbleached, all-purpose flour

2 1/2 tsp. baking powder

2 tbsp. granulated white sugar or sugar substitute, plus 1 tsp. for Berry Compote

2 large eggs

1 1/2 cups low fat milk or almond milk

Butter, for serving

Maple syrup, for serving

1 cup of your favorite frozen berries, like strawberries and blueberries or mixed berries

Instructions:

1. Add eggs and milk to a large mixing bowl and whisk until completely blended. Fold in remaining ingredients and whisk until there are only a few small lumps remaining.

2. Grease the inner pan.

3. Pour the batter into the inner pan; be sure not to fill it too high as the pancake will get stuck to the lid.

4. Lock the rice cooker lid in place. Set to WHITE RICE for 45 minutes.

5. While pancake is cooking add berries, 1 tsp. sugar, and 1 cup water in a small saucepan. Cover and cook on medium heat for 10 minutes, shake the pan to stir but do not uncover the pot.

6. Insert a toothpick into the pancake, when it removes cleanly the pancake is done. Remove the pancake by flipping the inner pan upside down over a large plate.

7. Remove Berry Compote from stove top and stir with a spoon to make sure it's at the desired thickness.

8. Top pancake with butter, syrup and berry compote. As a Gluten Free Alternative: Use your favorite gluten-free flour or recipe and enjoy!

Nutritional Info: Calories: 390, Sodium: 99mg, Dietary Fiber: 3.5 g, Fat: 6.4 g, Carbs: 67.9 g, Protein: 13 g.

Rice Cooker Summer Vegetable Frittata

Summer vegetables can really help you start the day out right when combined and a beautiful vegetable frittata. This is a great way to pack in an extra serving of vitamin and nutrient-rich veggies when it comes to your rice cooker and warmer. You will fall head over heels for this delicious dish and really transform breakfast.

Servings 2-4
Cook time

Ingredients

6 large eggs

1 tsp. milk

2 tbsp. parmesan cheese shaved

2 tsp. olive oil

1/3 cup sweet onion, diced

1 small carrot, diced

1 small red bell pepper, diced

1 small zucchini, diced

1/8 tsp. garlic powder

1/8 tsp. sea salt

1/8 tsp. black pepper

Instructions

1. Heat a frying pan to medium and add 1 tsp. olive oil. Add vegetables, season with salt, pepper, and garlic. Cook for 10 minutes.

2. Whisk eggs and milk in a mixing bowl until yolks are well incorporated with egg whites. Fold in parmesan.

3. Add egg mixture to the greased inner pan. Add the vegetables and distribute them evenly in the egg mixture with a spatula.

4. Select WHITE RICE. Serve immediately with your favorite juice, sparkling water or hot beverage.

Nutritional Info: Calories: 195, Sodium: 349mg, Dietary Fiber: 1.4 g, Fat: 12.6 g, Carbs: 7 g, Protein: 14.5 g.

Hard Boiled Eggs

Go protein powder house with these delicious hard-boiled eggs that are easy to whip up in no time. Serve delicious hard boiled eggs with a side of wheat toast and jam, creamy high protein yogurt or even use them in salads or as an afternoon snack. No matter how you like your hard boiled eggs these eggs are done in no time.

Servings 1
Cook Time 18 minutes

Ingredients

2 eggs   *2 cups water*

Instructions

1.   Pour the water into the inner pan.

2.   Add 2 eggs to inner pan and place in the rice cooker.

3.   Lock lid in place. Select MIXED key and cook for 15 minutes.

4.   Transfer eggs to an ice bath of cold water for 1 to 3 minutes. Peel, and enjoy!

5.   Note: you can cook 1 to 12 eggs in the Zojirushi Rice Cooker and Warmer, so the recipe can be changed depending on how many eggs you need.

Nutritional Info: Calories: 126, Sodium: 137mg, Dietary Fiber: 0 g, Fat: 8.8g, Carbs: 0.7 g, Protein: 11.1 g.

Sausage and Grits Breakfast Casserole

Go completely Southern with breakfast and whip up this delicious breakfast casserole packed with savory sausage and creamy grits. This is one that the whole family will enjoy for weekend family meals or something you can quickly cook for overnight guests. Pair it with fresh baked biscuits, coffee or tea, and orange juice and you've got one seriously amazing breakfast.

Servings 6
Cook time 1 hour 10 minutes

Ingredients

2 cups water

1/2 cup quick grits

1/2 tsp. sea salt

1 tbsp. butter

1/2 tsp. black pepper

1/8 tsp. garlic powder

1/2 lb. breakfast sausage, cooked and crumbled

1 cup white cheddar cheese, shredded

2 eggs

1/4 cup milk

Instructions

1. Add the water, grits, and salt to the inner pan of the rice cooker and stir to combine.

2. Lock the lid in place and cook on WHITE RICE for 30 minutes.

3. Add eggs and milk to a small mixing bowl. Beat with a whisk until well combined and set aside away from direct heat.

4. Turn the rice cooker OFF.

5. Open the lid and stir the grits; get the bottom with a spatula to ensure grits aren't stuck.

6. Stir in the butter until melted.

7. Fold in the remaining spices, cooked sausage, and cheese.

8. Fold the egg mixture into the grit mix and over again and lock the lid into place.

9. Select FLASH RICE and cook for 15 minutes; when the setting turns to warm turn the rice cooker OFF, open the lid, and stir.

10. Lock lid back into place and set to FLASH RICE for 15 additional minutes.

11. Serve immediately with your favorite breakfast beverage when the second cooking cycle is done!

Nutritional Info: Calories: 262, Sodium: 598mg, Dietary Fiber: 0.2 g, Fat: 20.6g, Carbs: 4.2 g, Protein: 14.6 g.

Whole Grain Porridge

Start your day off with a hearty whole grain breakfast and cook up this delicious whole grain porridge. Whole grain porridge is scrumptious when topped with your favorite dried fruits, nuts, or even honey and milk.

Servings 4
Cook Time 55 minutes

Ingredients

1/2 cup wild rice

1/2 cup steel-cut oats

1/2 cup wheat cereal

1 (2-inch) slice of an orange peel

1 cinnamon stick

2 tsp. light brown sugar or brown sugar substitute

1/4 teaspoon sea salt

1/4 cup dried cranberries, cherries, raisins or chopped apricots

Chopped nuts, serving

Honey, for serving

Milk or milk substitute like Coconut milk, for serving

Instructions

1. Add rice, oats, and wheat cereal to the inner pan.

2. Stir in the orange peel, cinnamon stick, sugar, sea salt, dried fruit, and 5 cups of filtered water.

3. Lock the lid and program the DELAY TIMER on BROWN RICE for 12 hours; remember this has a 50-minute cooking time, so include that in the calculation of what time you want to serve breakfast.

4. Add milk if desired and serve the whole grain porridge warm topped with nuts and honey.

Nutritional Info: Calories: 225, Sodium: 134 mg, Dietary Fiber: 3.1 g, Fat: 4.6 g, Carbs: 38.6 g, Protein: 6.9 g.

Huevos Rancheros

If you are craving a Savory breakfast dish, these huevos rancheros are the way to go! A classic Mexican Cuisine, huevos rancheros combined spice, creamy cheese, and delicious baked eggs for a real breakfast treat.

Servings 6-8
Cook time 40 minutes

Ingredients

1 tbsp. butter

10 eggs, beaten

1 cup light whipping cream

1 1/2 cups Mexican blend cheese, shredded

1/2 tsp. pepper

1/2 tsp. chili powder

1/2 tsp. garlic powder

1/2 tsp. cumin powder

Pinch of nutmeg

1 (4 oz.) can green chiles, drained

1 (10 oz.) can red enchilada sauce

1/2 cup cheddar cheese, shredded

8 tortillas, warmed

Instructions

1. Grease the inner pan with the butter.

2. Combine eggs, cream, Mexican cheese, and spices in a large mixing bowl.

3. Fold in the chiles and pour into the inner pan.

4. Lock lid into place and cook on WHITE RICE for 30 minutes.

5. Remove lid and top with enchilada sauce and cheddar cheese. Replace lid and cook an additional 15 minutes or until cheese is melted.

6. Top tortillas with huevos and serve immediately with your favorite breakfast drink!

Nutritional Info: Calories: 327, Sodium: 719 mg, Dietary Fiber: 1.9 g, Fat: 22.6 g, Carbs: 15.8 g, Protein: 15.9 g.

Slow-Cooked Blueberry French Toast

When your sweet tooth is calling at breakfast, this slow-cooked blueberry French toast will hit the spot. Serve it with scrambled eggs, sausage, bacon, orange juic or mimosas for one full breakfast full of delicious delights.

Servings 12
Cook time 1 hour

Ingredients

Non-stick cooking spray

8 large eggs

1/2 cup plain yogurt

1/3 cup sour cream

1 tsp. vanilla extract

1/2 tsp. ground cinnamon

1 cup milk or milk substitute

1/3 cup maple syrup

1 loaf of French or Italian bread, cubed

1 1/2 cups fresh or frozen blueberries

12 ounces cream cheese, cubed

Maple syrup, for serving

Instructions

1. Add eggs, yogurt, sour cream, vanilla, and cinnamon to a large mixing bowl; stir to combine. Gradually whisk in milk and maple syrup until blended.

2. Grease the inner pan of the rice cooker with cooking spray. Add half the cubed bread to inner pan; layer with half of the blueberries, cream cheese, and egg mixture. Add a second layer of bread cubes, then the other half of the blueberries, cream cheese, and egg mixture.

3. Cover and refrigerate overnight.

4. Remove French Toast from the refrigerator 30 minutes before cooking. Place inner pan in the rice cooker. Lock lid and set to MIXED key for 1 hour or until a knife inserted in the center comes out clean.

5. Serve with maple syrup and enjoy!

Nutritional Info: Calories: 220, Sodium: 166mg, Dietary Fiber: 0.6g, Fat: 15.3 g, Carbs: 15.9 g, Protein: 8.1 g.

Western Omelette Quiche

A taste of the Southwest, this delicious western omelette is a great way to get a full serving of veggies before you start your day. Packed with bell peppers, and cheddar cheese, you can even add in your own favorites like summer squash and zucchini to really make this omelette even more healthy.

Servings 4-6
Cook time 40 minutes

Ingredients

6 large eggs, well beaten

1/3 cup half and half

1/8 tsp. sea salt

1/8 tsp. ground black pepper

1/8 tsp. chili powder

1/8 tsp. garlic powder

1/2 cup ham, diced

1/2 cup bell peppers, diced

1/4 cup sweet onion, diced

3/4 cups cheddar cheese, shredded

Instructions

1. Add 1 1/2 cups of water to the inner pan. Butter or spray an 8-inch souffle dish and set aside. Whisk together the eggs, half and half, and spices in a large mixing bowl.

2. Add diced ham, peppers, onions, and cheese to the soufflé dish and stir to mix well. Pour egg mixture over to the top of the veggies and ham, and stir to combine.

3. Cover the souffle dish with a silicone lid or aluminum foil loosely. Use the aluminum foil to create a sling and lower the souffle dish into the inner pan of the rice cooker.

4. Lock the rice cooker lid in place and select BROWN RICE for 30 minutes. Open the lid, lift out the souffle dish and remove the foil carefully.

5. Serve immediately with an iced tea or cup of coffee!

Nutritional Info: Calories: 175, Sodium: 436mg, Dietary Fiber: 0.7g, Fat: 12.3 g, Carbs: 3.8 g, Protein: 12.5 g.

9

LUNCH RECIPES

Steamed Dumplings with Asian Salad

An Asian delicacy often found in the heart of Chinatown, steamed dumplings are delicious way to enjoy lunch without the fat. You can serve these up with a traditional pot of green tea and side of broccolini to really enjoy an authentic lunch with a taste of Asia.

Servings 2
Cook Time 20 minutes

Ingredients

12 frozen dumplings

2 cups water

Sesame oil, for cooking and serving

Soy sauce, for serving

Instructions

1. Add water to the inner pan of the rice cooker.

2. Use a paper towel to apply a light coat of sesame oil to the surface of the inner pan.

3. Arrange the dumplings in a single layer in the inner pan and place the basket in the bowl of the rice cooker.

4. Lock the lid in place and select MIXED key for 20 minutes.

5. Open the rice cooker and let the dumplings rest for 5 minutes to allow the excess moisture on the surface of the dumplings to evaporate.

6. Remove the MIXED keying basket from the rice cooker and transfer the MIXED keyed dumplings to a serving tray. Serve with sesame oil and soy sauce for dipping and enjoy!

Nutritional Info: Calories: 1180, Sodium: 638mg, Dietary Fiber: 36.1g, Fat: 90.8 g, Carbs: 168.6 g, Protein: 78.5 g.

Rice Cooker Braised Chicken Wings

Braised chicken wings are just as easy to whip up in no time when you use your Zojirushi. Served in a delicious sweet and savory sauce, these chicken wings are sure to make lunch time something super special.

Servings 1-2
Cook time 35 minutes

Ingredients

12 chicken wings

1 tsp. honey

2 tbsp. sesame oil

1 tsp. rice wine

1 tbsp. fresh ginger, sliced

1/8 tsp. white pepper

2 tsp. dark soy sauce

1/2 tsp. sea salt

Instructions

1. Rinse the chicken wings thoroughly in cold water. Dry them with a paper towel.

2. Add remaining ingredients to a large mixing bowl and stir to combine well. Add chicken wings and toss to coat.

3. Add the chicken wings to the inner pan reserving half the sauce for later. Select WHITE RICE and cook 30 minutes.

4. Flip the wings after 30 minutes, add remaining sauce and cook an additional 45 minutes.

5. Serve with extra sauce or soy sauce as desired!

Nutritional Info: Calories: 723, Sodium: 653mg, Dietary Fiber: 1.4g, Fat: 51.8 g, Carbs: 28.5 g, Protein: 35.1 g.

Buddha Bowl

The Buddha bowl is a delicious one meal dish that is making waves in the foodie world. Traditionally vegetarian or vegan, you can also throw in your favorite proteins in order to really ramped up this gorgeous dish. However, we recommend you try it just as it is because you will feel so full afterwards you might not even need the protein.

Servings 2-4
Cook time 40 minutes

Ingredients

4 tablespoons extra-virgin olive oil, divided

1 large sweet potato, peeled and cut into 1 1/2-inch pieces

1 cup quinoa, rinsed and drained

1 large clove garlic, minced

1/2 teaspoon sea salt

2 small carrots, peeled and cut in half

1 stalk Chinese broccoli

4 cups chopped kale

2 cups water

1 tablespoon lime juice

1 (15 oz.) can chickpeas, drained and rinsed for garnish

unsalted pistachios, for garnish

1 whole avocado, sliced for garnish

Instructions

1. Heat 2 tablespoons of olive oil over medium heat in a large frying pan. Add sweet potato, broccoli, carrots, quinoa, garlic and sea salt. Cook, while stirring, until the garlic is fragrant; about 3 minutes.

2. Add the quinoa mixture to the inner pan of the rice cooker. Stir in kale and water.

3. Lock the lid in place and select WHITE RICE for 20 minutes.

4. Remove the lid and let stand for 5 minutes.

5. Combine the remaining 2 tablespoons of olive oil, and lime juice in a small mixing bowl. Divide the quinoa mixture among 2 to 4 bowls.

6. Top each portion with chickpeas, pistachios and sliced avocado. Drizzle with the lime dressing and serve!

Nutritional Info: Calories: 829, Sodium: 330mg, Dietary Fiber: 27.6g, Fat: 29.6g, Carbs: 116.3 g, Protein: 32.2 g.

Chipotle Chicken Bowls with Cilantro Lime Rice

Kick things up a notch at lunch and quickly prep these chipotle chicken bowls with cilantro lime rice to serve every day of the week. For those of you that normally pack a lunch to go, this is the perfect way to meal prep on the weekend. Enjoy it with a can of sparkling water and 100 calorie nut pack for full-on lunch fun.

Servings 4
Cook time 50 minutes

Ingredients

1 cup quinoa, rinsed and drained

1 cup water

1/8 tsp. kosher salt

1/2 tsp. ground cumin

pinch black pepper

1 tablespoon chipotle paste

1 cup medium salsa

1 lb. boneless, skinless chicken thighs

1 (15 oz.) black beans

1/4 tsp. sea salt

1 lime, juiced

2 tsp. olive oil

2 tbsp. chopped cilantro

1 cup halved cherry tomatoes, for serving

1 avocado, sliced, for serving

4 lime wedges, for garnish

Instructions

1. Add quinoa and water to the inner pan. Cook on WHITE RICE for 18 to 22 minutes, or until all the liquid is absorbed. Fluff with a fork. Stir in the lime juice, olive oil, and cilantro; set aside.

2. Combine the salt, cumin black pepper, chipotle, and salsa in a medium mixing bowl.

3. Add the chicken to the inner pan of the rice cooker and pour the salsa mixture over chicken. Cook on WHITE RICE for 20 minutes.

4. Add the black beans and cook an additional 2 minutes.

5. Transfer chicken and beans to a bowl.

6.   Equally distribute quinoa, chicken, and beans to each bowl. Top with cherry tomatoes and sliced avocado. Serve with lime wedges and enjoy.

Nutritional Info: Calories: 908, Sodium: 676mg, Dietary Fiber: 25.8g, Fat: 25.5g, Carbs: 110.5 g, Protein: 63.9 g.

Lemon Chicken with Zucchini Noodles

Bright and zesty these lemon chicken zucchini noodles are just the thing to hit the spot in the middle of the week. When you are craving something super comforting like pasta, zucchini noodles are the perfect substitute. You can have 5 cups of zucchini noodles versus your one cup of pasta and still feel full all day long.

Servings 3
Cook Time 20 minutes

Ingredients

8 boneless chicken thighs

1 tbsp. smoked paprika

1 tbsp. unsalted butter, divided

1 tsp. olive oil

3 cloves garlic, minced

1 cup chicken broth

1/4 cup Parmesan shaved

1 lemon, juiced

1 teaspoon dried thyme

1/2 cup baby spinach, chopped

2 cups zucchini noodles

Sea salt and freshly ground black pepper, to taste

Instructions

1.   Add all ingredients to the inner pan and stir. Place inner pan in the rice cooker, close

2.   lid, and select WHITE RICE. Allow cooking until rice cooker switches to KEEP WARM

3.   Remove and transfer to plates. Season with sea salt and black pepper. Serve immediately as a main course.

Nutritional Info: Calories: 908, Sodium: 676mg, Dietary Fiber: 25.8g, Fat: 25.5g, Carbs: 110.5 g, Protein: 63.9 g.

BBQ Pork Chops with Steamed Apples

The recipe that is sure to warm anyone's heart for lunch time, these barbecue pork chops with steamed apples are absolutely perfect. When you're watching your weight or sincerely trying to cut carbs this lunch is the way to go. Serve it with a side of steamed vegetables or a salad for a delicious treat.

Servings 4
Cook time 45 minutes

Ingredients

4 bone-in pork chops

2 tbsp. olive oil

BBQ Seasoning

BBQ sauce

1 1/2 cups chicken broth

1 apple, sliced

Instructions

1. Rub both sides of each pork chop with your favorite BBQ seasoning.

2. Select WHITE RICE and add olive oil to the inner pan. Brown each pork chop on both sides, one at a time, and transfer to a plate.

3. Add in chicken broth to inner pan; use a spatula to scrape the browned bits off the bottom of the pan.

4. Add pork chops to the inner pan with a 1/3 cup of the BBQ Sauce; reserve the rest for serving.

5. Add apple slices to the inner pan. Select MIXED key and cook 30 minutes.

6. Remove apples and transfer to a plate. Transfer pork chops to a baking sheet. Baste with remaining BBQ sauce and place under an oven broiler, on high, for 2-3 minutes to caramelize. Serve immediately.

Nutritional Info: Calories: 356, Sodium: 819mg, Dietary Fiber: 1.4g, Fat: 19.6g, Carbs: 12 g, Protein: 31 g.

Orange Chicken

When you can't quite let go of your favorite take out, we've brought it to your kitchen. You can meal prep orange chicken to take with you to work or to send to school with children in no time. If you're crunched for time at home, this is also the perfect dish because you can have it on the lunch table in 30 minutes or less.

Servings 6
Cook time 30 minutes

Ingredients

2 lbs. chicken thighs, cut into 1-2 inch pieces

2 tbsp. grapeseed oil

1 cup no sugar added orange juice, plus 2 tbsp.

1 tbsp. ginger, grated

3 cloves garlic, minced

1 tbsp. mirin

1/3 cup brown sugar or sugar substitute

1/4 cup soy sauce

1 tsp. red chili pepper

zest from 1 orange

2 tablespoons cornstarch

2 tablespoons orange juice

Instructions

1. Add the grapeseed oil and select BROWN RICE. Add chicken and sauté for 2-3 minutes, stirring constantly; cook until it just starts to get golden.

2. Transfer chicken to a plate and deglaze the pot with 1/4 cup orange juice and scrape chicken bits off with a spatula.

3. Add the remaining 3/4 cups of orange juice, minced garlic, ginger, soy sauce, brown sugar, mirin, orange zest and red chili flakes to the inner pan.

4. Stir gently until all the ingredients are combined and fold in the chicken.

5. Close lid and select MIXED key for 15 minutes.

6. Combine 2 tbsp. cornstarch with 2 tbsp. orange juice in a small mixing bowl: whisk until there are no lumps.

7.   Gently fold the cornstarch mixture into the inner pan. MIXED key an additional 3 minutes.

8.   Uncover and let the Orange Chicken stand for 5 minutes and serve over rice.

Nutritional Info: Calories: 407, Sodium: 754mg, Dietary Fiber: 0.4g, Fat: 15.9g, Carbs: 18.9 g, Protein: 45 g.

Mongolian Beef

Skip the unhealthy take out and prep Mongolian beef at home before work. This is another great way to meal prep at home before you run out for the week. The best part about this recipe is that you can have it done in 20 minutes or under and still be able to cook a whole meal for the family.

Servings 4
Cook time 20 minutes

Ingredients

1 1/2 lbs. Flank steak

3/4 cups soy sauce

1 tsp. garlic powder

1/8 tsp. white pepper

1/2 cup brown sugar or brown sugar substitute

1/4 cup water

1/2 teaspoon fresh ginger, minced

1 carrot, shredded

1 tablespoon grapeseed oil

3 tbsp. cornstarch

3 tbsp. Water

1 green onion sliced, for garnish

Instructions

1. Add the grapeseed oil and select BROWN RICE. Add the beef and sauté for 2 minutes, stirring constantly; cook until it just starts to brown.

2. Add the soy sauce, garlic powder, white pepper, brown sugar, water, ginger and carrot to inner pan.

3. Stir gently until all the ingredients are combined.

4. Close lid and select MIXED key for 15 minutes.

5. Combine 2 tbsp. cornstarch with 2 tbsp. water in a small mixing bowl: whisk until there are no lumps.

6. Gently fold the cornstarch mixture into the inner pan. MIXED key an additional 3 minutes.

7. Uncover and let the Mongolian Beef stand for 5 minutes and serve over rice, garnished with green onions.

Nutritional Info: Calories: 489, Sodium: 808mg, Dietary Fiber: 1.2g, Fat: 17.6g, Carbs: 29.8 g, Protein: 50.8 g.

Beef Gyros

Mediterranean meals are very healthy, and these beef Gyros are just the lunch for those who want something hearty but light. We recommend that you enjoy these delicious gyros with a side of hummus and carrot sticks or a summer salad to really serve something yummy for lunch.

Servings 4
Cook time 20 minutes

Ingredients

1 lb. beef tenderloin, thinly sliced

1 tsp. dried parsley

1 tsp, black pepper

1 tsp. sea salt

1/2 tsp. oregano

1/2 tsp. basil

1/3 cup red onion, sliced

2 cloves garlic, minced

1/2 cup beef or vegetable broth

1 tbsp lemon juice

Balsamic vinegar, for garnish

1 tsp. olive oil, plus more for garnish

4 whole wheat pitas, halved

Sliced tomatoes, for garnish

Sliced onions, for garnish

Sliced cucumbers, for garnish

Lettuce, for garnish

Fresh buffalo mozzarella, thin sliced, optional garnish

Instructions

1. Add 1 tsp. Olive oil to inner pan and heat on WHITE RICE for 2 min.

2. Add meat, seasoning, red onion, garlic to inner pan. Cook for 5 min.

3. Pour lemon juice and broth over the meat, stir, and lock lid into place.

4. Select MIXED key for 10 minutes.

5. Transfer meat to a plate; discard broth and red onion.

6. To assemble Gyros, stuff each pita half with a few slices of meat, lettuce, tomato, cucumber, onions, and mozzarella.

7. Drizzle with vinegar and olive oil and serve.

Nutritional Info: Calories: 601, Sodium: 976mg, Dietary Fiber: 5.2g, Fat: 19.8g, Carbs: 37.3 g, Protein: 67.2 g.

Garlic Drumsticks

Craig drumsticks are the perfect protein to add to any type of stone lunch. Finger foods are honestly one of the best lunches because they are easy and quick to prepare. You can serve these garlic drumsticks with veggies and hummus, a slice or two of your favorite cheese, and sliced apples or oranges for a full and beautiful lunch.

Servings 4-6
Cook time 24 minutes

Ingredients

8 chicken drumsticks

1/4 cup water

1 tsp. sesame oil

1/2 cup dark soy sauce

2 tbsp. honey

2 tbsp. mirin

2 garlic cloves, minced

1 tsp. fresh ginger, minced

1/2 sweet onion, chopped

Instructions

1. Add all of the ingredients to the inner pan of the rice cooker. Select MIXED key for 30 minutes.

2. Let chicken rest on WARM for 5 minutes before opening the pot.

3. Transfer the drumsticks a cookie sheet lined with parchment paper. Broil the chicken on high for 2 minutes on each side.

4. Transfer chicken to a platter and serve with leftover sauce in the rice cooker.

Nutritional Info: Calories: 155, Sodium: 602mg, Dietary Fiber: 0.3g, Fat: 4.3g, Carbs: 11.6 g, Protein: 17.2 g.

Tavern Burgers

Beefy delicious Tavern burgers are an absolute treat when it comes to lunch time. These delicious burgers will have all of your lunch time guests pulled into thinking they're in a gourmet restaurant. Serve them with delicious french fries or turnip fries for a fun lunchtime meal.

Servings 6-8
Cook time 20 minutes

Ingredients

2 lbs. lean ground beef

1 tsp. onion, finely chopped

1/2 tsp. sea salt

1/4 tsp. black pepper

1 tsp. Cajun seasoning

1 (10.75 oz) can tomato soup

Yellow mustard, for serving

Swiss cheese slices, for serving

Lettuce, for serving

Sandwich Buns, split, for serving

Instructions

1. Add ground beef, onion, sea salt, black pepper, Cajun seasoning and tomato soup to the inner pan. Cook on MIXED key for 30 minutes; let rest on KEEP WARM for five minutes.

2. Assemble sandwiches by spooning beef onto bottom slice of bun. Top with favorite toppings and serve hot!

Nutritional Info: Calories: 284, Sodium: 795mg, Dietary Fiber: 1.7g, Fat: 9.7g, Carbs: 9.9 g, Protein: 37.9 g.

Jacket Potatoes

Jacket potatoes can really hit the spot when it comes to lunch! You can top your jacket potatoes with anything your heart desires. We love ours with butter and sea salt, but you can also use shredded cheese, as well as baked beans or even tuna for a protein packed lunch.

Servings 4
Cook time 21 minutes

Ingredients

4 medium baking potatoes

Butter, for serving

Sea salt, for serving

Black pepper, for serving

Sour cream, for serving

Instructions

1. Fill the inner pan with 1 cup of water.

2. Prick your potatoes, all over, with a fork. Place them in a inner pan.

3. Lock the lid in place and set to MIXED key for 20 minutes.

4. Serve with sea salt, black pepper, butter and sour cream.

Nutritional Info: Calories: 144, Sodium: 143mg, Dietary Fiber: 2.4g, Fat: 1.8g, Carbs: 30.5 g, Protein: 3.6 g.

Egg Mayo Sandwiches

Elevate your egg Mayo sandwiches with this delicious recipe. The Zojirushi rice cooker is a great way to even quickly whip up your favorite sandwiches to Take On The Go. Pack these sandwiches for a perfect Saturday picnic or simply put them in the kids lunch bag as a healthy treat.

Servings 2
Cook Time 30 minutes

Ingredients

5 eggs

2 cups water

6 tbsp. mayonnaise

1/3 cup parmesan cheese shaved

1 tsp. mustard powder

1 tsp. parsley

1/8 tsp. Sea salt

1/8 tsp. Black pepper

Pinch of nutmeg

Pinch of brown sugar or sugar substitute

Four slices of your favorite bread or 2 baguettes

Instructions

1. Pour the water into the inner pan.

2. Add 5 eggs to inner pan and place in the rice cooker.

3. Lock lid in place. Select MIXED key and cook for 25 minutes.

4. Transfer eggs to an ice bath of cold water for 5 minutes.

5. Peel, and add to a large mixing bowl. Mash with a fork, and fold in remaining ingredients. Stir to combine well.

6. Top bread or stuff baguette with egg mayo; any remaining egg may be refrigerated for one day.

Nutritional Info: Calories: 489, Sodium: 802mg, Dietary Fiber: 1.3g, Fat: 27.5g, Carbs: 41 g, Protein: 20.2 g.

Pulled Chicken Tacos

Delicious tacos are right at your Mexican loving fingertips with the Zojirushi. You will quickly be able to make delicious chicken tacos that can also be put and put in your lunch bag for an on-the-go quick, hearty meal.

Servings 4-6
Cook time 35 minutes

Ingredients

4 boneless, skinless chicken thighs

1 tbsp. chili powder

1 tbsp. ground cumin

1 tsp. smoked paprika

1 tsp. dried oregano

1 tsp. garlic powder

1 tsp. sea salt

2 limes, juiced

1 cup chicken broth

6 corn tortillas

Lettuce, shredded for serving

Guacamole, for serving

Sour cream, for serving

Hot sauce, for serving

Cotija cheese, for serving

Instructions

1. Add chicken, spices, chicken broth and lime juice to the inner pan.

2. Cook on MIXED key for 25 minutes.

3. Remove chicken and pull using a fork to shred. Transfer chicken back to pot and cook for additional 5 to 10 minutes.

4. Remove chicken and discard broth.

5. Top tortillas with guacamole, chicken, lettuce, sour cream, cheese and hot sauce to serve.

Nutritional Info: Calories: 115, Sodium: 601mg, Dietary Fiber: 2.8g, Fat: 5.2g, Carbs: 15 g, Protein: 7.8 g.

Beefy Broccoli Noodles and Cheese

Comfort food cravings often hit in the middle of the day and these Beefy Broccoli Noodles really hit the spot. Loaded with gooey cheese, they are the perfect mid day comfort meal. Serve them with a glass of milk or almond milk to really hit your comfort spot.

Servings 4
Cook time 30 minutes

Ingredients

2 cups leftover beef roast, like London Broil

2 cups egg noodles

2 cups beef broth

1/2 tsp. sea salt

2 cups broccoli florets, chopped

1 cup milk or milk substitute like Almond

1 1/2 cups mozzarella cheese, shredded

Instructions

1. Combine the beef, broth, noodles, broccoli, and salt in the rice cooker. Lock lid in place and cook on WHITE RICE for 15 minutes.

2. Open the lid and fold in the milk and cheese.

3. Lock the lid and MIXED key and additional 10 minutes; when ready the cheese will be melted, and the milk well-incorporated.

4. Serve immediately and enjoy.

Nutritional Info: Calories: 306, Sodium: 768mg, Dietary Fiber: 2.1g, Fat: 8.8 g, Carbs: 27 g, Protein: 28.6 g.

Mango Cucumber Rice Salad

If you don't necessarily like to meal prep on the weekends, salads are a great way to meal prep the night before. Just remember to put your dressing in a separate container or on the bottom of your salad and mix it up when you get to work. The best part about this salad is the fact that it doesn't wilt!

Servings 6
Cook time 35 minutes

Ingredients

1 1/2 cups rice

1/2 cup quinoa, rinsed

2 cups water

Juice of 1 lime, plus 1 tsp. zest

2 tbsp. olive oil

1 tsp. sugar

1 tsp. coarse ground pepper

1 tsp. garlic powder

1 cup mango, diced

1 cucumber, peeled, seeded and diced

1 jalapeno, seeded and thinly sliced

1/3 cup chopped fresh cilantro

Instructions

1. Add rice, quinoa, and water to the inner pan. Select WHITE RICE and cook for 30 minutes.

2. Combine lime, zest, olive oil, sugar and spices in a large mixing bowl. Fold in mango, cucumber, jalapeno, and cilantro.

3. Fluff rice mixture with a fork and evenly distribute to bowls. Top with a large scoop of mango mixture and serve.

Nutritional Info: Calories: 292, Sodium: 10mg, Dietary Fiber: 2.5g, Fat: 6 g, Carbs: 53.9 g, Protein: 6 g.

10

SOUPS, CHILI, STEWS, SOUFFLES

Rice Cooker Chili

Hearty robust chili is a fan favorite for all things from tailgates to weekend parties, fun nights in with the family, and anytime you're really craving some spicy comfort food. There's delicious rice cooker chili is just the way to go when you want to kick things up in the comfort food department.

Servings 6-8
Cook time

Ingredients

1 lb. ground beef

1 (15 oz.) can chopped tomatoes, no-sodium added

1 (15 oz.) can pinto beans

1 (15 oz.) can red kidney beans, in chili sauce

1 tbsp. chili powder

1 cup tomato sauce

1/8 tsp. sugar

2 tsp. dried oregano

1 green bell pepper, diced

1 small onion, diced

Salt and pepper to taste

Instructions

1. Add ground beef to rice cooker and cook on MIXED key until browned; drain the excess fat.

2. Add remaining ingredients and MIXED key for 30 minutes to 1 hour.

3. Enjoy topped with cheese, sour cream, or additional diced onions. Alternatively, you can omit the beef for vegetarians and add lentils or swap the beef for turkey for a healthy choice.

Nutritional Info: Calories: 498, Sodium: 223mg, Dietary Fiber: 18.3g, Fat: 5.2g, Carbs: 72.8 g, Protein: 41.9 g.

Taco Soup

A lean alternative to traditional beef filled soup, is our delicious Taco Soup! You'll love the flavor explosion of this delicious soup that you can top with things like shredded cheese and tortilla chips. Don't be afraid to go even further and a dollop of sour cream or some pickled jalapeno peppers.

Servings 6
Cook time 1 hour

Ingredients

1 lb. chicken breast or tenders, diced

1 (15 oz) can hominy

1/2 medium onion, diced

1 clove garlic, minced

2 tsp. olive oil

5 cups chicken broth, low-sodium

1 (15 oz.) can diced tomatoes

1/2 cup brown rice

1/2 cup black beans, canned

Tortilla chips, for serving

Shredded cheese, for serving

Instructions

1. Add olive oil to inner pan and heat for 2 minutes on MIXED key; add onion and garlic and saute for 2 minutes.

2. Add diced chicken and brown for about 5 to 10 minutes.

3. Add remaining ingredients to the inner pan and cook on BROWN RICE for 45 minutes to 1 hour and serve topped with tortilla chips and shredded cheese.

Nutritional Info: Calories: 321, Sodium: 947mg, Dietary Fiber: 6.1g, Fat: 12.4g, Carbs: 38.8 g, Protein: 31.5 g.

White Chicken Chili

Creamy white chicken chili is another delicious healthy alternative to eating beef. This recipe will definitely spice things up in your house when you use your Zojirushi rice cooker. You can also garnish this delicious soup with oyster crackers or shredded mozzarella for an elevated bowl of soup that really hits the spot.

Servings 6
Cook time 25 minutes

Ingredients

1 lb. skinless boneless chicken thighs

5 cups chicken broth

2 garlic cloves, minced

1 medium onion, diced

1 (4.5 oz.) can green chiles

2 (15 oz.) cans can white northern beans, do not drain

1/2 tsp. dried oregano

1 tsp. ground cumin

1 tsp. chili powder

1 tsp. sea salt

1 tsp. ground black pepper

Instructions

1. Add all of the ingredients to the inner pan.

2. Cook on MIXED key for 25 minutes.

3. Carefully remove the chicken thighs, and use a fork and knife to shred the chicken.

4. Return chicken to the inner pan, and press MIXED key an additional 5 minutes.

5. Serve hot!

Nutritional Info: Calories: 209, Sodium: 902mg, Dietary Fiber: 5.1g, Fat: 4.2g, Carbs: 18.7 g, Protein: 23.4 g.

Chicken Daikon Soup

It's gorgeous alternative to homemade chicken noodle soup really hits the spot when you need a little bit of love. Soup is very comforting to the soul, and this delicious soup is full of comforting ginger that both aids in healthy immune systems and upset tummies. Packed full of delicious vegetables this soup also gives you loads of nutrients and vitamins.

Serves 2-3

Cook Time 3 hours

Ingredients

1 lb. boneless, skinless chicken thighs

1 tsp. ginger, freshly sliced

1 daikon, peeled and cut into large chunks

1 small carrot, peeled and shredded

8 shiitake mushrooms, sliced and stems removed

1 tbsp. goji berries

3 conpoy or dried scallops

1/8 tsp. sea salt

Instructions

1. Add 4 cups of water to the inner pan and choose MIXED key for 10 minutes; discard liquid and set aside blanched chicken pieces.

2. Add another 4 cups of water to the rice cooker pot. Add chicken and remaining ingredients.

3. Lock the lid in place and MIXED key for 45 minutes; allow to simmer for 1 hour on KEEP WARM when the MIXED key cycle is done.

4. Enjoy hot!

Nutritional Info: Calories: 448, Sodium: 783mg, Dietary Fiber: 5.4g, Fat: 12.2g, Carbs: 33.9 g, Protein: 52.5 g.

Hearty Red Wine Stew

For those who love to cook with red wine this is the recipe for you! This hearty, delicious stew is full of herbs and rustic vegetables that really hit the spot. You'll love this hearty red wine stew all year around when it comes to feeding your family. Enjoy it with crusty bread and sangria for a weekend treat!

Servings 6-8

Cook time 2 hours

Ingredients

2 pounds beef chuck, cut into 1 1/2 inch cubes

2 tbsp. all-purpose flour

1 tsp. garlic powder

1 tsp. sea salt

1 tsp. black pepper

1 tbsp. olive oil

3 shallots, peeled and quartered

1lb. small red potatoes halved

3 medium carrots, sliced large

3 sprigs fresh thyme

2 sprigs fresh rosemary

1 (15 oz.) can petite diced tomatoes

1 tbsp. balsamic vinegar

1 cup red wine

2 cups low-sodium beef broth

Instructions

1. Toss the beef cubes with the flour, garlic powder, salt and pepper to coat.

2. Add the all of the ingredients and toss well to combine.

3. Set to MIXED key for 2 hours.

4. Ladle the stew into bowls and serve with your favorite, fresh bread.

Nutritional Info: Calories: 296, Sodium: 443mg, Dietary Fiber: 1.8g, Fat: 9g, Carbs: 11.1 g, Protein: 36.6 g.

Butternut Cauliflower Soup

Creamy butternut squash and earthy cauliflower really do blend well for one scrumptious soup. When it comes to winter weather favorite, this soup is sure to make your list. Serve it with a delicious toasted baguette and butter or a salad for a full, flavorful meal.

Servings 6
Cook time 40 minutes

Ingredients

1 onion, diced

1 tsp. olive oil

3 garlic cloves, minced

1 lb. cauliflower, chopped

1 lb. butternut squash, cubed

2 cups chicken or vegetable broth

1/4 tsp. nutmeg

1/2 tsp. dried thyme

1/2 tsp. red pepper flakes

1/4 tsp. sea salt

1/2 cup half and half

1/2 cup sour cream

shredded cheddar cheese, for serving

crumbled bacon, for serving

sour cream, for serving

Instructions

1. Set to MIXED key and add olive oil and onion; cook 5 minutes. Add garlic and cook 2 minutes.

2. Fold in cauliflower, butternut squash, broth, and spices.

3. Cook on MIXED key for 25 minutes.

4. Add half and half and sour cream to inner pan. Use an immersion blender to cream the soup or allow soup to cool and blend in batches in a food processor or blender until smooth.

5. Top with cheese, bacon, and additional sour cream and serve.

Nutritional Info: Calories: 301, Sodium: 343mg, Dietary Fiber: 3.9 g, Fat: 16.3g, Carbs: 17.2 g, Protein: 23.2 g.

Pho

Pho is another fan favorite these days a month the true Foodies. This delicious soup is just as easy to make it home in your rice cooker and warmer as it is to order from a takeout restaurant. Serve it for your favorite guests at a dinner party for some sincerely sweet dinner party fun - just don't forget the rice wine and saki!

Servings: 2-4
Cook time 1 hour 10 minutes

Ingredients

4 lb. of beef bones

2 medium onions, sliced in half

2 cloves garlic, peeled and halved

2 medium carrots, sliced in half

1/2 cup fresh ginger

1 tbsp. apple cider vinegar

1 tsp. ground cinnamon

1 tsp. ground coriander

1 tsp. whole black peppercorns

2 tsp. sea salt

4 whole star anise

6 cups of water

Add-ins:

1 cup bean sprouts

1/2 lb. sirloin steak, sliced very thinly

1 lime, cut into wedges

2 scallions, sliced thinly

1 package of rice noodles

1 tbsp. fresh cilantro or mint

Fresh Hot Red Pepper, sliced

Instructions

1. Bring water to boil in the rice cooker. Add the bones and cook for 5 minutes.

2. Place onion, garlic, carrot, and ginger on a greased sheet-tray. Broil in the oven for 10 minutes, or until charred.

3. Add charred veggies, apple cider vinegar, spices, and more water, if needed, to cover the bones in the inner pan.

4. Lock lid in place and MIXED key for 45 minutes. After cycle turns to KEEP WARM leave to rest, covered, for 15 minutes.

5.   Cook the rice noodles by package instructions and set aside until ready to eat.

6.   Strain the broth through a mesh strainer until it runs clear; about 3 times. Discard bones and veggies.

7.   Return broth to inner pan on MIXED key for 5 minutes.

8.   Distribute bone broth, evenly into bowls, add in desired toppings, and enjoy!

Nutritional Info: Calories: 325, Sodium: 939mg, Dietary Fiber: 15.9 g, Fat: 3.1g, Carbs: 70.2 g, Protein: 9.3 g.

Beef and Guinness Stew

If you're looking for something to serve that's authentic for St Patrick's Day, this is the recipe for you. Cooking with craft beer and stouts has become a fan favorite in recent years. This Beef and Guinness Stew is sure to hit the spot no matter what kind of food do you are!

Servings 8
Cook time 2 hours

Ingredients

1 lbs. stew beef, 1-inch pieces

salt and pepper to season

2 tsp. olive oil

1 small sweet onion, chopped

1 tsp. garlic powder

2 large carrots, peeled and chopped into thick slices

4 red potatoes, quartered

2 celery stalks, chopped into thick pieces

1/4 cup plain flour

2 cups stout beer, like Guinness

3 tbsp. tomato paste

2 cups beef broth

1 tsp. dried thyme

Instructions

1. Season beef generously with salt and pepper.

2. Heat olive oil in the inner pan and add beef; MIXED key until browned. Transfer to a plate.

3. Add onion and sauté 5 minutes. Add the carrots, celery, and potatoes, and cook for an additional 5 minutes. Stir the flour into the vegetables in the inner pan and coat them evenly. Cook, stirring occasionally, for an additional 3 minutes.

4. Gently fold the Guinness into the stew; mix well to dissolve flour, then add the tomato paste, broth and thyme, scraping off any browned bits on the bottom of the inner pan with a wooden spoon or spatula.

5. Select MIXED key to cook for 5 minutes. Fold the beef back into the pot cover and cook 1 hour.

Nutritional Info: Calories: 235, Sodium: 297mg, Dietary Fiber: 3 g, Fat: 5.2g, Carbs: 26.4 g, Protein: 17 g.

Creamy Tomato Soup

Comfort food lovers will literally fall head over heels for this creamy tomato soup. Our favorite way to do comfort food tomato soup is to serve it with a grilled cheese, but you can also have it with a salad to make it even more healthy.

Servings 6
Cook time 25 minutes

Ingredients

3 shallots, peeled and halved

1 tbsp. olive oil

3 carrots, peeled and chopped

1 (15 oz.) can tomato sauce

1 (15 oz.) can stewed tomatoes

1 tbsp. tomato paste

1 cup vegetable broth

1 tsp. oregano

1/4 tsp. sea salt

3 oz. half and half

salt and pepper to taste

Instructions

1. Add olive oil, shallots and carrot to inner pan and MIXED key for 5 minutes.

2. Add remaining ingredients and set to MIXED key for 20 minutes.

3. Add the half and half to the soup and puree using an immersion blender until smooth; alternatively, allow to cool and use a food processor or blender to smooth in small batches.

4. Top with parmesan crisps or serve with your favorite soup crackers!

Nutritional Info: Calories: 94, Sodium: 610mg, Dietary Fiber: 2.9 g, Fat: 4.5g, Carbs: 11.8 g, Protein: 3.3 g.

Beef Barley Soup

Hearty barley meets beef in a delicious vegetable stock for one seriously amazing soup when you cook up this recipe. You'll get a fully packed portion of veggies, protein and bone broth that will stick to your ribs with whole grains.

Servings 6-8
Cook time 1 hour 30 minutes

Ingredients

1 lb. stew meat

Sea salt and pepper, to season stew meat

1 tsp. olive oil

10 key mushrooms, quartered

1/2 cup onion, chopped

1/2 cup celery, chopped

1/2 cup carrots, chopped

6 garlic cloves, minced

6 cups beef or vegetable broth

1 cup water

2 bay leaves

1/2 teaspoon dried thyme

2/3 cups pearl barley, rinsed

Instructions

1. Season the stew meat with sea salt and pepper. Heat olive oil in the inner pan on MIXED key. Add the stew meat and brown on all sides for about 3-5 minutes.

2. Add remaining ingredients and lock lid into place.

3. MIXED key for 20 minutes, serve and enjoy!

Nutritional Info: Calories: 222, Sodium: 188mg, Dietary Fiber: 3.4 g, Fat: 7.7g, Carbs: 17.4 g, Protein: 20.3 g.

Potato Leek Soup

A British winter time favorite, potato and leek soup is perfect as an appetizer or even a main meal. Creamy and robust this soup is sure to bring warmth into your home. As a main meal we love this soup with a grilled Edam cheese sarnie or white cheddar topped crackers.

Servings 6-8
Cook time 30 minutes

Ingredients:

1 leek, white and light green parts only, rinsed and diced

2 tbsp. olive oil

2 cloves garlic, minced

1/2 tsp. sea salt

1/2 tsp. black pepper

1/4 teaspoon thyme

Pinch of nutmeg

3 small baking potatoes, peeled and diced

3 cups chicken or vegetable broth

1/4 cup half and half

1/4 cup sour cream

Instructions

1. Add the leek, olive oil, garlic, salt, pepper, thyme, nutmeg, broth, and potatoes to the inner pan and MIXED key for 30 minutes.

2. Add half and half and sour cream. Blend with an immersion blender until smooth, and garnish with additional black pepper.

Nutritional Info: Calories: 191, Sodium: 166mg, Dietary Fiber: 1.2g, Fat: 7.6g, Carbs: 14 g, Protein: 17.2 g.

11

DESSERTS

Self-Saucing Banana Pudding

Self-saucing banana pudding is the perfect dessert for the person on the go. That's because you don't have to whip up an icing or create anything else to go with this dessert. Rich and decadent, the whole family will fall in love with this masterpiece.

Servings 6-8
Cook time 1 hour

Ingredients

1 cup caster sugar

1 1/2 cups self-raising flour, sifted

1/3 cup butter, melted and cooled

1 tsp. vanilla extract

1/4 cup mashed banana

1 egg, lightly beaten

3/4 cups milk

1/2 cup packed brown sugar

1/8 tsp. nutmeg

1 tsp. cinnamon

2 1/2 cups boiling water

ice cream, to serve

Instructions

1. Preheat rice cooker to MIXED key for 10 minutes.

2. Grease the inner pan with butter using wax paper.

3. Combine the first 7 ingredients above in a large mixing bowl; whisk until well-combined.

4. Fold into the inner pan. Sift sugar, nutmeg, and cinnamon over the pudding mix.

5. Spoon the boiling water gently and evenly over the mixture.

6. Lock lid in place and cook on MIXED key for 1 hour.

7. Serve hot with a scoop of ice cream on top!

Nutritional Info: Calories: 324, Sodium: 85mg, Dietary Fiber: 1g, Fat: 9.9g, Carbs: 56.6 g, Protein: 4.3 g.

Chocolate Lava Cake

We had to include the chocolate lovers when it comes to this delicious recipe. If you sincerely love chocolate, this chocolate lava cake is something that is positively to die for! Chocolate lovers will not be able to get enough of this cake especially when it's served with a dollop of vanilla bean ice cream.

Servings 6-8
Cook time 1 hour 10 minutes

Ingredients

1 box of Devil's Food Chocolate Cake mix, prepared according to box instructions

1 (15 oz.) can of milk chocolate frosting, divided

Non-stick cooking spray

Instructions

1. Spray the inner pan of the rice cooker with cooking spray.

2. Add cake batter prepare as instructed on box.

3. Spoon half of the chocolate frosting into the middle of the cake batter.

4. Cook on MIXED key for 1 hour.

5. Flip the inner pan upside down over a cake plate. Heat the remaining frosting in a microwave for 25 seconds, and pour over the warm cake, and serve.

Nutritional Info: Calories: 197, Sodium: 229mg, Dietary Fiber: 2g, Fat: 22.6g, Carbs: 77 g, Protein: 0.3 g.

Banana Bread

Banana bread is a warm delicious treat that can be served as dessert or even breakfast. The perfect brunch treat, we just love banana bread. Just make sure the bananas you use are extra ripe!

Servings 6-8
Cook time 1 hour 10 minutes

Ingredients

1 1/2 cup unbleached flour

1/2 cup sugar or sugar substitute

2 tsp. baking powder

1/2 tsp. baking soda

1/2 tsp. vanilla extract

1/2 tsp. sea salt

1 cup ripe bananas, mashed

1/3 cup softened butter

1/4 cup milk

1 egg

1/4 cup walnuts, chopped

Instructions

1. Combine the flour, sugar, baking powder, baking soda and salt in a large mixing bowl; whisk until the ingredients are well mixed.

2. Fold in the bananas, butter, milk, egg and vanilla extract. Use an electric mixer to mix until the batter has a uniform thick consistency.

3. Fold in chopped walnuts.

4. Grease the bottom of the inner pan with non-stick cooking spray.

5. Pour batter into inner pan and cook on WHITE RICE for 1 hour. Transfer to plate and let cool for one hour before serving.

Nutritional Info: Calories: 187, Sodium: 259mg, Dietary Fiber: 2.1g, Fat: 8.7g, Carbs: 38.2g, Protein: 7.2 g.

Poached Pomegranate Spiced Pears

Transform your holiday dessert table with this delicious recipe. You can show off your culinary skills by barely lifting a finger this holiday. Sweet, ripe pears delicately spiced are the perfect thing to serve at your next winter party.

Servings 4
Cook time 55 minutes

Ingredients

2 firm Anjou or Bosc pears, peeled, halved, and cored

2 cups pomegranate juice

2 cups apple cider

2 cinnamon sticks

1 large orange peel, about 1 inch thick

2 whole cloves

1 pinch of freshly shaved nutmeg

1 piece fresh ginger peeled, cut into thin slivers

Instructions

1. Add all ingredients to the inner pan of the rice cooker.

2. Lock the lid and cook on WHITE RICE for 50 minutes, or tender when a fork is inserted. Open the lid and flip the pears over; let rest for 1 hour. Turn pears over again and let sit for another hour.

3. Serve warm or refrigerate overnight for a more intense flavor and color.

Nutritional Info: Calories: 745, Sodium: 146mg, Dietary Fiber: 7.5g, Fat: 2.8g, Carbs: 185.5g, Protein: 2.8 g.

Rice Cooker Tatin Cake (Apple Upside Down Cake)

Summer sweet apples are the star of this delicious dessert. We love this quick rice cooker Titan cake topped with a dollop of heavy cream and caramel sauce.

Servings 4
Cook time

Ingredients

2 apples, peeled and cut into 8 wedges

2 tbsp. butter, plus 3 tbsp. melted

3 tbsp. sugar, plus 1/4 cup

Olive oil

1/2 cup all-purpose, unbleached flour

1 tsp. baking powder

Pinch of salt

2 eggs

Instructions

1. Heat 2 tbsp. butter in a nonstick pan and add the apples; toss to coat and cook for about 5 minutes.

2. Add 3 tbsp. sugar, gently stir to combine and cook until caramelized.

3. Grease the inner pan with a drop of olive oil and add the apples to cover the bottom of the inner pan.

4. Mix all-purpose flour, 1/4 cup sugar, baking powder, salt, 3 tbsp melted butter and the two eggs together, and pour the batter over the apples.

5. Cook on WHITE RICE for 60 to 90 minutes; or until firm.

6. Allow it to cool in the inner pan for 20 minutes after cooking.

Nutritional Info: Calories: 205, Sodium: 113mg, Dietary Fiber: 3.2g, Fat: 11.8g, Carbs: 37.1g, Protein: 4.7 g.

Green Tea Matcha Cake

Green tea matcha cake is sure to warm any baker at heart! Matcha exploded on the foodie network a few years ago, and we think you'll fall in love with this delicious recipe that is just as delicate as green tea.

Servings 4-6
Cook time 1 hour 30 minutes

Ingredients

2 large eggs

1 cup unbleached flour

1/2 cup sugar

1/2 cup butter

1 tbsp. green tea matcha powder

1/2 teaspoon baking powder

Instructions

1. Combine all of the ingredients in a large mixing bowl

2. Grease the inner pan of the rice cooker with non-stick cooking spray.

3. Set to WHITE RICE for 1 hour 30 minutes.

4. Transfer to a plate to cool for 20 minutes and serve!

Nutritional Info: Calories: 305, Sodium: 133mg, Dietary Fiber: 2.9g, Fat: 17.2 g, Carbs: 32.9g, Protein: 6.8 g.

Rice Pudding

Warm your soul and your foodie loving heart with some delicious rice pudding when you use your Zojirushi to make rice pudding. This delicious rice pudding can even be served with a sprinkle of cinnamon to really sweet and things up!

Servings 2 - 4

Cooking time 25 minutes

Ingredients

2 cups Jasmine rice, uncooked

5 1/2 cups milk

1/3 cup sugar

1 tsp. vanilla extract

1 tsp. sugar

1/4 cup unsweetened coconut, shredded

Diced mango, for serving

Instructions

1. Add the rice and milk to the inner pan of the rice cooker and stir to combine.

2. Lock the lid in place and set to WHITE RICE.

3. When the Keep Warm cycle turns on, open the rice cooker, and add the sugar and vanilla; stir until well-combined.

4. Return lid and set for a second WHITE RICE cycle. Stir every 15 to 20 minutes until the desired consistency is reached.

5. Fold in the coconut. Serve warm with diced mango on top.

Nutritional Info: Calories: 624, Sodium: 160mg, Dietary Fiber: 5.8g, Fat: 8.9 g, Carbs: 119.4g, Protein: 17.9g.

Lemon Lime Polenta Cake with Yogurt Icing

Lemon and lime come together to really brighten up a beautiful polenta cake topped with creamy yogurt icing. A sincerely sweet treat, this dessert is best served after a really hearty meal because it is so bright and light. Perfect for weekend brunch with a sangria or mimosa bar!

Servings 6-8
Cook time 45 minutes

Ingredients

7/8 cups almond flour

1 2/3 sticks butter

1/2 cup polenta

1 1/2 tsp. baking powder

Pinch of salt

3 eggs

2 lemons

1 lime

1 tsp. vanilla extract

1 cup vanilla yogurt, for icing

1 cup icing sugar, for icing

Instructions

1. Beat butter and sugar together in a mixing bowl until creamed. Fold in eggs. Next, fold in almond flour, salt, and polenta.

2. Remove the beaters and zest the limes and lemons directly into the bowl. Add the juice of 1 lemon and the lime.

3. Stir well to combine; fold the mixture into a greased inner pan and smoothing it out on top.

4. Cook on WHITE RICE for about 30-35 minutes, or until a toothpick inserted comes out clean. Set the inner pan with cake aside to cool for 20 minutes.

5. Prepare to ice by mixing yogurt and sugar together in a small mixing bowl; refrigerate to set until cake is cool. Drizzle cake with icing and serve.

Nutritional Info: Calories: 354, Sodium: 204mg, Dietary Fiber: 1.6 g, Fat: 24.6 g, Carbs: 29g, Protein: 6.4g.

Chocolate Fondue

Transform your dinner parties with a beautiful chocolate fondue that is fun to share with everyone around the table. Chocolate fondue is also super-quick, yet decadent and delicious, and is perfect with after dinner tea or coffee.

Servings 10-20
Cook time 10 minutes

Ingredients

1/2 cup water

1/2 cup half and half

1 tbsp. honey

1/4 tsp almond extract

6 oz. 70% cacao, grated

3 oz. milk chocolate, grated

1 cup of strawberries

1 cup apples, sliced

1 cup Angel Food Cake, cubed

1 cup brownies, cubed

Instructions

1. Combine the first 4 ingredients in the rice cooker on MIXED key for about 5 minutes.

2. Fold in chocolate and stirring until all chocolate is melted and mixture turns glossy; about 5 minutes.

3. Keep warm to serve with strawberries, apples, angel food cake, brownies or whatever you love to dip in Chocolate Fondue!

Nutritional Info: Calories: 89, Sodium: 56mg, Dietary Fiber: 1.7 g, Fat: 8.5 g, Carbs: 16.4g, Protein: 2.1g.

Japanese Mochi

When you're trying to watch your sugar, this is the perfect sweet treat for you. Japanese Mochi are a delicious dessert made from sweet brown rice that offers you the perfect hint of sweet when served alone - or alongside creamy ice cream.

Servings 4-6
Cook time 11 hours 10 minutes

Ingredients

1 cup sweet brown rice

1/8 tsp. salt

1 part cornstarch, for dusting

1 part cocoa powder, for dusting

Ice cream, for serving

Instructions

1. Soak the rice in water overnight. Drain off excess water and process the rice until it makes a smooth, creamy paste in a food processor or blender.

2. Add to the inner pan of the rice cooker, lock the lid in place, and MIXED key for 10 minutes until rice is glutinous sticky and glossy.

3. Combine cornstarch and cocoa powder. Dust a cookie sheet with the powder mixture.

4. Pour the hot mochi mixture onto the cookie sheet evenly; let cool for 30 minutes; then, refrigerate for 2 hours.

5. Cut the sheet of mochi into 2-inch squares and bake at 450 degrees Fahrenheit for about 10 minutes; the mochi will puff so don't be alarmed when they change shape.

6. Serve warm with a scoop of ice cream.

Nutritional Info: Calories: 219, Sodium: 349mg, Dietary Fiber: 1.4 g, Fat: 8.5 g, Carbs: 46.3g, Protein: 2.8g.

Easy Flan

Creamy custard meets delicious caramel in this beautiful easy flan that you can make right in your Zojirushi. A traditional Spanish dessert, Flan is the perfect complement to any meal when served with coffee or a coffee cocktail - or even a tawney port for those who dare to be decadent.

Servings 3-5
Cook time 1 hour 10 minutes

Ingredients

6 egg yolks

1 (12 oz.) can evaporated milk

1 (12 oz.) can condensed milk

1 tsp. pure vanilla extract

1/4 cup granulated sugar, for caramel sauce

One flan molder

Instructions

1. Gently combine the egg yolk, condensed milk, evaporated milk and vanilla in a large mixing bowl and set aside.

2. Add granulated sugar to a saucepan and heat on a stove at medium-low; turn off the heat and assemble flan.

3. Pour the custard into the flan molder. Add caramel sauce evenly over custard. Place flan in the inner pan.

4. Lock lid in place and set to MIXED key for one hour. Let it cool completely, transfer to a plate, and serve!

Nutritional Info: Calories: 414, Sodium: 168mg, Dietary Fiber: 0 g, Fat: 16.1 g, Carbs: 54.7g, Protein: 13.3g.

12

KID-FRIENDLY RECIPES

Chili Mac

When you combine the Savory Taste of chili with macaroni, you have one sincerely amazing meal when it comes to the kids. Chili mac is where comfort meets comfort and gives the kids something to beg you to cook!

Servings 4-6
Cook time 30 minutes

Ingredients

1 lb. lean ground round beef

2 tbsp. chili powder

1 tsp. garlic powder

2 cups water

1 (15 oz.) can diced tomatoes

1 (15 oz.) can red kidney beans, in chili sauce

2 cups elbow macaroni

1 cup cheddar cheese, shredded

Instructions

1. Preheat the rice cooker on MIXED key for five minutes. Add beef and sauté until browned; breaking it up with a wooden spatula while cooking.

2. Stir in the chili powder and garlic powder.

3. Add the water, tomatoes, red kidney beans, and pasta.

4. Lock lid in place and cook for one WHITE RICE cycle.

5. Serve immediately, topped with cheese.

Nutritional Info: Calories: 1081, Sodium: 358mg, Dietary Fiber: 13.4 g, Fat: 53.3 g, Carbs: 69.1g, Protein: 81.3g.

Mac N' Cheese

Kids love a good mac n' cheese and this one will have them wanting to be your Mini-Chef assistant in the kitchen. Ooey gooey Mac and Cheese has never been so easy with a one pot Zojirushi.

Servings 4
Cook time 50 minutes

Ingredients

2 cups elbow macaroni

1 tsp. sea salt

1 (12 oz.) can evaporated milk

3/4 cups cheddar cheese, shredded

3/4 cups shaved parmesan cheese

3/4 cups mozzarella melting cheese, like Velveeta Shreds

1/2 teaspoon mustard powder

1/2 teaspoon freshly ground black pepper

2 tbsp. Butter

Salt and pepper, to taste

Instructions

1. Combine the macaroni, salt and 2 cups water in the rice cooker. Set on WHITE RICE and cook for 30 minutes and water is absorbed.

2. Fold in the butter, milk, cheese, salt, and pepper.

3. Lock the lid, turn the rice cooker to the KEEP WARM and let cook, stirring occasionally for 10 minutes. Serve warm!

Nutritional Info: Calories: 497, Sodium: 818mg, Dietary Fiber: 1.6 g, Fat: 25.8 g, Carbs: 41.9g, Protein: 24g.

Spaghetti and Meatballs

When you're looking to cook some family favorites in your Zojirushi this recipe is for you! You can have a beautiful family dinner on the table in under 30 minutes when you whip up one pot spaghetti and meatballs any night of the week.

Servings 4
Cook Time 20 minutes

Ingredients

1 (15 oz.) can of Italian Sauce or marinara

3 1/2 cups water

1/2 lb. spaghetti pasta

1 lb. frozen meatballs (1/2 inch size)

1 tsp. garlic powder

1 tsp. dried Italian herbs

Parmesan cheese, for serving

Garlic toast, for serving

Instructions

1. Combine all ingredients in the inner pan.

2. Lock lid in place and set to WHITE RICE for 20 minutes.

3. Serve immediately with parmesan cheese and garlic toast.

Nutritional Info: Calories: 497, Sodium: 818mg, Dietary Fiber: 1.6 g, Fat: 25.8 g, Carbs: 41.9g, Protein: 24g.

Applesauce

Applesauce is the perfect dessert or healthy snack for your kids. All kids love applesauce, right? You don't have to buy store-bought anymore when you cook it up in your Zojirushi.

Servings 4-6
Cook time 30 minutes

Ingredients

4 large apples, peeled, cored and chopped

2 tsp. sugar

1/4 cup unfiltered apple juice

3/4 tsp. ground cinnamon

Instructions

1. Add all ingredients into the inner pan of the rice cooker.

2. Lock lid in place and cook on WHITE RICE for 25 to 30 minutes.

3. Puree with hand blender or food processor and serve warm or chill in refrigerator overnight in a resealable container.

Nutritional Info: Calories: 89, Sodium: 1 mg, Dietary Fiber: 3.8 g, Fat: 0.3 g, Carbs: 23.6 g, Protein: 0.5 g

Baked Beans

A classic picnic or grilling side, baked beans are also one of the most delicious dishes that you can fix up for the children in your Zojirushi. Serve these delicious beans with hot dogs, potato salad, macaroni salad, and potato chips for an All-American summertime feast.

Servings 4-6

Cook time 35 minutes

Ingredients

1 1/2 cups dry pinto beans

1 cup warm water

2 tbsp. olive oil

1 medium sweet onion, finely diced

1/4 teaspoon salt

1 tsp. garlic powder

1 (15 oz.) can tomato sauce

2 tbsp. ketchup

1 tbsp. brown sugar

1/2 teaspoon paprika

1/8 teaspoon nutmeg

2 bay leaves

Instructions

4. Add dried beans to a large bowl and fill up with double the water. Mix in a teaspoon of salt and soak overnight. Strain and rinse; add to inner pan.

5. Add remaining ingredients to inner pan, lock lid in place and set to WHITE RICE for 35 minutes. Test bean texture, if not cooked to desired softness continue cooking in 10-minute increments until done.

6. Serve alone or with your favorite cookout food!

Nutritional Info: Calories: 245, Sodium: 532 mg, Dietary Fiber: 9.1 g, Fat: 5.5 g, Carbs: 39 g, Protein: 11.7 g

---

Corn On The Cob

Yummy, delicious corn on the cob with butter and salt really hits the spot. Kids will love helping you cook this super easy side dish or snack when it comes to the Zojirushi.

Servings 3-6
Cook time 25 minutes

Ingredients

3 ears of corn, husked and rinsed, cut in half

Butter, for serving

Salt, for serving

Instructions

1. Fill the inner pan with 2 cups water.

2. Place corn on the cob in the inner pan; insert basket into the rice cooker.

3. Lock lid and MIXED key for 25 minutes.

4. Enjoy with butter and salt to taste!

Nutritional Info: Calories: 83, Sodium: 12 mg, Dietary Fiber: 2.1 g, Fat: 2.8 g, Carbs: 14.5 g, Protein: 2.5 g

---

Bacon Ranch Potatoes

Kids can be picky when it comes to eating. These delicious bacon ranch potatoes will help your kids transform any meal into something that I absolutely love! Spiced and everything nice is what you'll get with these fun potatoes.

Servings 6

Cook time 25 minutes

Ingredients

2 lb. red potatoes, rinsed and cleaned, cut into 1-inch pieces

3 bacon strips, cut into pieces

2 tsp. dried parsley

1 tsp. garlic powder

1 cup cheddar cheese, shredded

1 package ranch dressing seasoning

Instructions

1. Add potatoes, bacon and 1/4 cups of water into the inner pan of rice cooker.

2. Stir in parsley and garlic powder.

3. Set to WHITE RICE for 25 minutes; check potatoes. Add additional water if need to cook longer.

4. Transfer potatoes to a mixing bowl and combine with ranch dressing and cheese; serve immediately.

Nutritional Info: Calories: 257, Sodium: 306 mg, Dietary Fiber: 2.6 g, Fat: 13.2 g, Carbs: 25.3 g, Protein: 9.8 g

---

Sloppy Joes

When you are pressed for time and really need a great meal for the family, sloppy joes are a great addition to our weekly meals. Simply throw all of the ingredients into your Zojirushi and you'll have saucy sandwiches the kids love in less than an hour.

Servings 6
Cook time 35 minutes

Ingredients

2 lbs. lean ground beef

1 small onions, diced

1 small green bell pepper, diced

1 tsp. garlic powder

2 tsp. cumin

2 tsp. paprika

1 tsp. salt

1/2 tsp. black pepper

1 (15 oz) can tomato sauce

2 tbsp. tomato puree

2 tsp. apple cider vinegar

2 tsp. molasses

2 tsp. yellow mustard

1 tsp. ketchup

6 sandwich buns

Instructions

1. Brown beef in a skillet over medium heat. Drain. Combine all ingredients in the inner pan of the rice cooker and MIXED key for 30 minutes.

2. Let rest for 5 minutes to set.

3. Spoon onto sandwich buns and serve with your favorite sides!

Nutritional Info: Calories: 456, Sodium: 1052 mg, Dietary Fiber: 3.2 g, Fat: 12.4 g, Carbs: 31 g, Protein: 53.6 g

Homemade Chicken Soup

When you are looking to whip up a family favorite in no time, homemade chicken soup really hits the spot. You can cook hearty, warm chicken soup in less than an hour! Perfect for lunch or dinner, this chicken soup gets an A+ with the kids.

Servings 8
Cook time 35 minutes

Ingredients

2 carrots, peeled and sliced

2 celery stalks, trimmed, rinsed and sliced

1 small yellow onion, peeled and diced

5 garlic cloves, peeled and diced

2 quarts chicken broth

1 cup water

2 tablespoons apple cider vinegar

2 cans chicken, drained

1 package egg noodles

Instructions

1. Add all ingredients to the inner pan.

2. Lock lid in place and set to WHITE RICE for 30 minutes.

3. Leave on KEEP WARM for 5 minutes or until ready to serve. Serve with grilled cheese or your favorite soup crackers.

Nutritional Info: Calories: 133, Sodium: 802 mg, Dietary Fiber:0.9 g, Fat: 2.9 g, Carbs: 9 g, Protein: 16.3 g

Pizza Pasta

Ordering pizza can be super expensive for your family, but you can bring back pizza night with this delicious dish. Pizza pasta will have the whole family asking for seconds. While this recipe calls for traditional toppings - you can add any of your favorites to explore all the possibilities this easy dish has to offer.

Servings 4-6
Cook time 35 minutes

Ingredients

1 tbsp. olive oil

2 (8 oz.) jars of pizza sauce

3 1/2 cups water

1 (8 oz.) package mozzarella cheese shredded

1 cup pepperoni slices

2 cups macaroni

2 tsp. garlic powder

1 tsp. Italian seasoning

Instructions

1. Combine olive oil, pasta, water and 1 jar of pizza sauce in the inner pan. Cook on MIXED key for 15 minutes.

2. Fold in the additional jar of sauce, half of the cheese and half pepperoni. Cook on MIXED key for an additional 10 minutes.

3. Top with remaining cheese and pepperoni; Cook on MIXED key for 5 minutes or until cheese is melted and serve.

Nutritional Info: Calories: 294, Sodium: 670 mg, Dietary Fiber: 2.3 g, Fat: 11.1 g, Carbs: 32 g, Protein: 14.4 g

---

Lasagna

When you don't have time to bake the perfect lasagna, your Zojirushi will come in handy. That's because of the fact that rice cookers are amazing for one pot meals just like lasagna. Serve it with some crusty bread and a salad for one hearty Italian meal at home.

Servings 6
Cook time 30 minutes

Ingredients

1 (16 oz.) package pasta, like ruffles or spirals

1 cup ricotta cheese

1 cup mozzarella cheese

1 lb. ground beef

1 (32 oz.) jar pasta sauce

4 cups water

Instructions

1. Add beef to inner pan and brown ground beef on MIXED key until cooked through.

2. Add pasta, sauce, and water; cook on MIXED key for 20 minutes.

3. Stir in Ricotta cheese and half the mozzarella.

4. Pour into a baking pan and top with the rest of the mozzarella.

5. Broil for 2-3 minutes in an oven or until cheese is melted and serve.

Nutritional Info: Calories: 560, Sodium: 774 mg, Dietary Fiber: 3.9 g, Fat: 14.6 g, Carbs: 64.5 g, Protein: 40.2 g.

Pizza Pull-Apart Bread

Pizza pull-apart bread is another answer to take away Pizza. You can serve this one up for after-school snacks or as a delicious lunch with some carrot sticks or celery sticks. Your kids will love helping you make this delicious pull-apart bread for loads of family fun.

Servings 4-6
Cook Time 10 minutes

Ingredients

2 cans pizza dough, like Pillsbury

1/3 cup olive oil

2 cups mozzarella cheese

1 tsp. garlic powder

1/4 cup parmesan cheese, grated

4 cloves garlic minced

1 package of mini pepperonis

pizza sauce, for serving

Instructions

1. Cut pizza dough into 1-inch strips.

2. Toss all ingredients in a large mixing bowl using your hands.

3. Add 1 cup of water to the bottom of your inner pan.

4. Place dough in a springform pan and place over water in the inner pan.

5. Cook on MIXED key for 15 minutes. Let stand on KEEP WARM for 5 minutes and serve with pizza sauce for dipping.

Nutritional Info: Calories: 222, Sodium: 282 mg, Dietary Fiber: 0.4 g, Fat: 4.8 g, Carbs: 16.1 g, Protein: 6.6 g.

Chili Dogs

Another kids fan-favorite is the chili dog! You can whip them up in less than 10 minutes when you use your Zojirushi. Served on toasted hot dog buns with your favorite toppings, these dogs are outta this world!

Servings 4-8
Cook time 9 minutes

Ingredients

1 package uncured hot dogs

1 package hot dog buns

1 (10 oz.) can hot dog chili

Ketchup, for serving

Mustard, for serving

Instructions

1. Add hot dog chili to inner pan. Add hot dogs to the inner pan, and place above the inner pan.

2. Lock lid in place and MIXED key for 5-7 minutes.

3. Assemble dogs in buns and top with chili, ketchup, and mustard.

Nutritional Info: Calories: 114, Sodium: 314 mg, Dietary Fiber: 0.7 g, Fat: 4.8 g, Carbs: 14.8 g, Protein: 3.2 g.

Made in the USA
Monee, IL
31 August 2024

64983046R00104